THE
NEED
FOR
CREEDS
TODAY

THE
NEED
FOR
CREEDS
TODAY

Confessional Faith in a Faithless Age

J. V. FESKO

Baker Academic
a division of Baker Publishing Group
Grand Rapids, Michigan

© 2020 by J. V. Fesko

Published by Baker Academic
a division of Baker Publishing Group
PO Box 6287, Grand Rapids, MI 49516-6287
www.bakeracademic.com

Printed in the United States of America

Library of Congress Cataloging-in-Publication Data
Names: Fesko, J. V., 1970– author.
Title: The need for creeds today : confessional faith in a faithless age / J. V. Fesko.
Description: Grand Rapids, Michigan : Baker Academic, a division of Baker Publishing Group, 2020. | Includes bibliographical references and index.
Identifiers: LCCN 2020018361 | ISBN 9781540962591 (paperback) | ISBN 9781540963543 (casebound)
Subjects: LCSH: Creeds—History and criticism.
Classification: LCC BT990 .F47 2020 | DDC 238—dc23
LC record available at https://lccn.loc.gov/2020018361

21 22 23 24 25 26   7 6 5 4 3 2

Dedicated to the memory
of
R. C. Sproul

Contents

Acknowledgments

Sometimes a speaker develops material, creates notes, and then builds an outline for a lecture. But whenever I can, I write essays (or chapters) from which I then create lecture outlines. I am grateful for the invitations from the Texas Area Association of Reformed Baptist Churches (TAARBC) and the Southern California Reformed Baptist Pastors' Conference (SCRBPC) to lecture on confessions. Their invitations prompted me to write this book and afforded me the occasion to reflect more deeply on the topic of confessions as I investigated and documented their biblical warrant, rich Reformed heritage, ideological foes, and great benefit to the church.

I am grateful to Dave Nelson and the publishing team at Baker. Thank you for supporting this project and for your tremendous care and professionalism in seeing this book through to publication. Thanks to Alex DeMarco for all of his careful editorial suggestions and corrections.

I am also grateful to the board, faculty, and staff at Reformed Theological Seminary, Jackson, Mississippi. I am privileged to be part of an institution that steadfastly believes and promotes the historic Reformed faith, which is contained in the Scriptures and summarized in our confessions and catechisms.

And I also want to say thank you to my family. Your support, love, and kindness throughout the years enable and encourage me to continue to read, research, and write.

When I was a recent college graduate, I sensed a call on my life to serve in ordained ministry. At the time, I was a theological neophyte and was looking for good books to read. One of my friends who was working on his PhD in church history started taking me through Calvin's *Institutes*. This was definitely a huge uphill climb; my brain ached with each step up the slopes of Calvin's two-volume magnum opus. I had to keep a notecard handy with one-word synonyms for many of the words I encountered. Also at this time, another good friend of mine was continually mentioning and quoting another theologian when he taught the Bible to my college and career Sunday school class.

My parents noted the name and bought me several of his books for Christmas. As I read this theologian, I could tell that deep currents of thought ran through the pages of his books, but they were still accessible. The books poured forth a steady stream of surging water, but I could get close enough to the water's edge to take regular sips. He made complex concepts easier to understand, and I soaked in vast reservoirs of theological knowledge. I soon found myself attending his conferences and buying as many of his audio cassette sermons and lectures as I could. Even though I had a hefty reading schedule in seminary, I found time to read this theologian's books. I worked in the evenings as a janitor in the library and would listen to his tapes three to four hours a night, five days a week. With his more advanced lectures, I had to make frequent stops by the colossal Oxford English Dictionary to look up the polysyllabic word grenades that he would throw into his lectures. But the more I listened, the more I liked, the more I learned, and the more I came to love the Reformed faith. God used this theologian to produce a crisis in me that caused me to fully embrace the Reformed faith and to join the Orthodox Presbyterian Church.

December 14, 2017, was a bittersweet day. It was the day that this beloved theologian, pastor, teacher, and friend, R. C. Sproul, died and met his Maker face-to-face. I miss him. Through his books and tapes, he was my theological mentor. Although Dr. Sproul's death leaves a hole in modern-day theology, his absence should remind us that Christ is faithful. The Lord continues to build his church, and the gates of hell will never prevail against it. Christ continues to send his gifts to his church: faithful ministers of the gospel to teach and preach the message of salvation. I give thanks to Christ for giving us so many ministers over the ages—faithful servants who regularly feed us the manna from heaven. For these reasons, I dedicate this book on confessions of faith to the memory of R. C. Sproul. May God raise up scores of zealous ministers to herald the Reformed faith.

Introduction

Within the American religious psyche, there is an antipathy and distrust of tradition. Ralph Waldo Emerson (1803–82) embodied this negative disposition: "Our age is retrospective. It builds the sepulchers of the fathers. It writes biographies, histories, and criticism. The foregoing generations behold God and nature face to face; we, through their eyes."[1] Instead of looking at religion through the eyes of our predecessors, Emerson believed individuals should look on revelation with their own eyes: "Why should not we also enjoy an original relation to the universe? Why should not we have a poetry and philosophy of insight and not of tradition, and a religion by revelation to us, and not the history of theirs? . . . There are new lands, new men, new thoughts. Let us demand our own works and laws and worship."[2] But Emerson's conception of religion was decidedly different from the faith of his forebears. Nature was, for him, the chief book in the divine library, and its mystical message was something that refused to be captured in propositions.[3] Clouding revelation with propositions would make the savant unpoetic.[4] Moreover, reading books was for idle times. When a person can read God directly, "the hour is too precious to be wasted in other men's transcripts of their readings."[5]

1. Ralph Waldo Emerson, "Nature," in *Essays & Lectures* (New York: Library of America, 1983), 7.
2. Emerson, "Nature," 7.
3. Emerson, "Nature," 40.
4. Emerson, "Nature," 43.
5. Ralph Waldo Emerson, "The American Scholar," in *Essays & Lectures*, 58.

We are each, therefore, our own priest as we eschew the thoughts of others in favor of directly reading God through nature. Rather than deriving knowledge from other great minds, the truly mature person must discover that the fountain of all good is found within.[6] Emerson sowed seeds that spawned a negative view of traditions, creeds, and Scripture and a positive view of individuals forming their own religious outlooks for themselves. Prayers and the dogmas of the church were merely historical markers that showed how high the waters of faith once rose.[7] The church's dogmas were not supposed to be permanent boundary markers to distinguish orthodoxy from heterodoxy. To this end, Emerson opines, "Yourself a newborn bard of the Holy Ghost—cast behind you all conformity, and acquaint men at first hand with Deity."[8] These sentiments struck a chord with a number of American scholars and theologians. Emerson influenced a new generation of Unitarian theologians;[9] and American jurist and Supreme Court justice Oliver Wendell Holmes Jr. (1841–1935) submitted that Emerson's lecture "The American Scholar" was "our intellectual Declaration of Independence."[10] Emerson cast the die, and American religion would bear these characteristics for generations to come.

Harold Bloom (1930–2019) documented the American religious phenomenon as individualistic and mystical: Jesus is not a first-century Jew but a contemporary American who also happens to be the first person to be resurrected from the dead. As a trailblazer, he shows others the way to salvation. Bloom notes the problem: "What was missing in all this quite private luminosity was simply most of historic Christianity." Now, in all fairness, Bloom celebrated this doctrinal evolution.[11] Nevertheless, Bloom's observation confirms that 150 years later, Emerson's style of individualistic religion still thrives. Injected with the steroids of revivalism, American religion has

6. Ralph Waldo Emerson, "The Divinity School Address," in *Essays & Lectures*, 78.

7. Emerson, "Divinity School Address," 85.

8. Emerson, "Divinity School Address," 89.

9. Gary Dorrien, *The Making of American Liberal Theology: Imagining Progressive Religion 1805–1900* (Louisville: Westminster John Knox, 2001), 58–80.

10. Oliver Wendell Holmes Jr., *Ralph Waldo Emerson* (Boston: Houghton Mifflin, 1886), 115.

11. Harold Bloom, *The American Religion*, 2nd ed. (New York: Chu Hartley, 2006), 54.

produced an ahistorical brand with celebrities that have transcended their own denominational trappings. Charles Finney (1792–1875) was supposedly a Presbyterian, and Billy Graham (1918–2018) claimed to be a Southern Baptist, but both gave little attention to the doctrinal distinctives of their respective denominations.[12] Bloom notes, unsurprisingly, that American religion tends to eschew a sense of the communal.[13] And Americans have only accelerated down the individualism highway in the age of the internet.

Technology has propelled levels of individualism to increasingly greater heights. Psychologist Jean Twenge writes of the latest generation to come of age, which she calls "iGen."[14] This generation comprises one-quarter of the American population, and they are disengaging from religion at alarming rates. In the 1960s, 93 percent of college students affiliated with a religion; that figure had dropped to 68 percent by 2016. Among iGen'ers, disavowing religious beliefs is more socially acceptable than it was for previous generations.[15] Their generation tends to look at ancient religious texts as merely the creations of fallible human beings, and they generally think that whatever of value religion might offer appears elsewhere with less baggage.[16] Today's young people are radically individualized and willing to carve out their own private religious beliefs or to rest content in deliberate, blissful ignorance. One of the reasons that participation in organized religion is on the decline is the "American culture's increasing focus on individualism," the idea that people can and should make their own choices.[17] In a technological world where the average life span of a smartphone app is less than thirty days, what hope is there that iGens will open ancient books and engage texts that go back thousands of years, or that they will embrace traditional religion?[18]

12. Bloom, *American Religion*, 63.
13. Bloom, *American Religion*, 56.
14. Jean M. Twenge, *iGen: Why Today's Super-Connected Kids Are Growing Up Less Rebellious, More Tolerant, Less Happy—and Completely Unprepared for Adulthood* (New York: Atria Books, 2017).
15. Twenge, *iGen*, 121–22.
16. Twenge, *iGen*, 122–23.
17. Twenge, *iGen*, 138.
18. Kevin Kelly, *The Inevitable: Understanding the 12 Technological Forces That Will Shape Our Future* (New York: Penguin Books, 2017), 11.

In such a context, a book on the importance of confessions of faith might seem dead on arrival. But first impressions are not always accurate. As we look back on the development of American religion, we can say that the use of confessions of faith has been in decline overall, yet there are two important factors that we should consider. First, in spite of the rise of religious individualism, a minority of Christians has continued to employ confessions of faith. This minority includes Christians of all stripes, but my own interests and loyalties lie with Reformed Christianity. This branch of Christianity stands in the theological tradition that emerged from the sixteenth-century Reformation and has been codified in the Westminster Standards (including the Confession and the Larger and Shorter Catechisms) and the Three Forms of Unity (the Belgic Confession, the Canons of Dort, and the Heidelberg Catechism). Second, if we take a step back and look at the big picture of the last two thousand years of church history, such a perspective quickly reveals that confessional Christianity has dominated the scene. The rise of individualism in the last two hundred years is anomalous. This is not to say that individualism will soon fade away like the morning mist. But the church has historically employed confessions of faith, and that trend will continue. Still, given the rise of individualism, we presently stand at a crossroads where we must reassess and refamiliarize ourselves with the biblical necessity and the practical virtues of confessions of faith.

Argument and Plan of the Book

Argument

This book defends the thesis that confessions of faith are therefore necessary for both the being (*esse*) and the well-being (*bene esse*) of the church. In other words, confessions of faith are not merely beneficial or wise, and thus helpful to the church (although they certainly are these things). Rather, the Bible teaches that the church should create its own confessions of faith in order to pass on to future generations the faith once delivered to the saints. Such a claim might seem indefensible, especially in our present climate of hyperindividualism. Nevertheless, the historical witness of the last two thousand years of church history and the widespread use of confessions of faith by Western and Eastern churches, Protestant and Roman Catholic, ancient and contemporary, confirm the validity of this thesis.

Plan

The first chapter explores eight biblical texts, demonstrating that the Bible instructs the church to create confessions of faith. When God told the Israelites to tell future generations the meaning of the Passover, he commanded parents to catechize their children in Israel's faith. They had a divinely given *traditio* that they were supposed to pass down from generation to generation. God also gave to Israel a basic confession of faith in the Shema, "Hear, O Israel: The LORD our God, the LORD is one" (Deut. 6:4). This confession was a guardrail against heterodoxy, a statement of doctrinal truth upon which Israel was supposed to meditate, a confessional truth that inspired love and devotion to God. The apostle Paul picks up these themes in his Pastoral Epistles when he rehearses his "trustworthy sayings," statements that the early church created based on the teaching of Jesus. The church was not supposed to mimic Christ's teaching but to soak it in and to pass it down to future generations so that they too would love God and one another. Love lies at the heart of a biblically subordinated confessionalism.

The second chapter rehearses the history of confessions in the Reformed tradition from 1500 to 1700. Since the nineteenth century, many Reformed theologians have believed that post-Reformation confessions distorted the theology of the Protestant Reformation with their increasingly detailed, scholastic approaches. As common as this criticism has been, this chapter demonstrates that the post-Reformation confessions stand in continuity with their Reformation-era predecessors. The differences between the confessions of the two periods lie in the rise of intra-Protestant disputes and in debates with Roman Catholics. The confessions of both eras are also different because they arose under different historical circumstances and because the later confessions were written by committees of theologians rather than by individual Reformers. As greater numbers of theologians contributed, increased precision as well as deliberate doctrinal ambiguity was necessary to accommodate at times conflicting views.

In other words, even though critics often characterize confessions as doctrinal straitjackets, in addition to drawing lines to mark the boundaries between true and false doctrine, those drafting these confessions also drew circles to make room for multiple views within the bounds of orthodoxy.

The third chapter considers why confessions of faith have largely fallen into disuse in the American ecclesiastical scene. It touches on some of the present-day reasons confessions have been neglected, but it also delves into the sixteenth century for deeper answers. The sixteenth-century Reformation holds the seeds of both confessionalism and anticonfessionalism. Doctrinal skepticism was used as an engine of theological warfare, and it quickly grew out of control and contributed to the Enlightenment devaluation of tradition and to the wholesale rejection of confessions of faith. But the blame for anticonfessionalism does not lie exclusively in the hands of critics; proponents of confessions shoulder some of the blame. Theological conviction and violence went hand in hand; one of history's most brutal conflicts was fought along confessional lines, Protestant versus Catholic, and this too contributed to the large-scale rejection of confessions of faith. If it is going to put confessions to proper use, the church must own up to past abuses and take measures to ensure that the same errors do not arise in the future.

The fourth chapter addresses a number of the benefits of confessions of faith. Complementing the first chapter, which largely deals with confessions and the *esse* (being) of the church, this chapter explores how confessions serve the church's *bene esse* (well-being). Confessions of faith serve as boundary markers to distinguish orthodoxy from heterodoxy, create room for a diversified orthodoxy, and connect the church to its historic witness. That is, confessions allow the church to practice what G. K. Chesterton (1874–1936) called the "democracy of the dead"; this is the idea that, when trying to decide a difficult question, we should not merely consult the living; wisdom dictates that we also consult the dead by means of old books and, I would add, confessions.[19] The church did not begin when you or I

---

19. G. K. Chesterton, *Orthodoxy: The Romance of Faith* (1908; repr., New York: Doubleday, 1990), 48.

joined its ranks; it has existed for millennia. Throughout that time, Christ has given teachers to the church as gifts, and we ignore them at our own peril (Eph. 4:11–12).

The fifth chapter examines a little-known episode in church history when a delegate to the Synod of Dort (1618–19) challenged a colleague to a duel to the death over a doctrinal disagreement. This chapter shows that even when engaged in the most sacred of tasks, such as writing a confession of faith, the church has at times allowed the world to mold the church into its own likeness, thereby shaping its conduct in sinful ways. The "duel that almost was" serves as a perennial warning. We must not allow the contaminants of sin to infect either the confessions or the confession-writing process as we seek to pass down the faith once delivered to the saints. Again, confessions of faith are not about cold doctrinal precision but about ensuring that the church preserves the faith so that we can love our triune God and our neighbors and pass the truth down to future generations.

The book then concludes with summary observations about the importance of confessions of faith for the future of the church.

Conclusion

Sometimes truth sounds strange, even hostile to our sensibilities. This may be the case for us as we encounter the church's confessions of faith from within our individualistic culture. Nevertheless, there are good biblical reasons for creating and passing down confessions of faith. When we create, profess, and pass confessions down to future generations, we do not propagate the dead faith of the living but the living faith of the dead.[20] We practice the "democracy of the dead" and join hands with the saints from ages past to give witness to the lordship of the triune God and the redemption that comes through the gospel of Christ.

---

20. Jaroslav Pelikan, *The Vindication of Tradition* (New Haven: Yale University Press, 1984), 43.

ONE

Biblical Arguments for Confessions

Introduction

As democracy spread throughout the burgeoning United States of America in the eighteenth and nineteenth centuries, ideals of freedom and Christianity mingled and gave birth to a decidedly American form of religion. Barton W. Stone (1772–1844), Thomas Campbell (1763–1845), and Thomas's son Alexander Campbell (1788–1866) were leaders of the Restoration movement (also known as the Stone-Campbell movement), which wanted to peel back the layers of accumulated dogma and return Christianity to what they believed was its purest, most primitive form. The movement leaders referred to their break with the Presbyterian church as their "declaration of independence." And Alexander Campbell encouraged his followers to commemorate July 4, 1776, as a day equal to the Jewish Passover. That is to say, Stone and the Campbells created a populist movement that rode on the winds of American democracy and freedom. Instead of confessions of faith, the Stone-Campbell movement trumpeted the motto "no creed but the Bible." It was clear that many in the new world had little space for confessional, old-world faith.[1] The anti-creedal movement grew as those churches that embraced theological democracy outpaced their confessional competitors. In 1776, Congregationalist and Presbyterian churches were dominant, holding almost 40 percent of the American churchgoing population. But by 1850, about 54 percent of American churchgoers were attending Baptist and Methodist churches, with Presbyterian and Congregationalist churches together claiming only about 15 percent of the pie.[2] The sentiment that creeds and confessions were unbiblical, and thus to be rejected, thrived in the nascent nation. Considering how popular the "no creed but the Bible" mentality was and continues to be, we must ask, What does the Bible have to say about confessions?

At first blush, such a question might seem absurd. Some might ask, What does the Spirit-inspired Bible have to do with these all-too-human documents? But closer examination shows that there is biblical evidence to support the claim that confessions of faith are both biblical and necessary. To prove this claim, this chapter surveys eight biblical texts: the institution of the Passover liturgy (Exod. 13:14–15), the giving of the Shema (Deut. 6:4–6), the apostle Paul's five "trustworthy sayings" (1 Tim. 1:15; 3:1; 4:7–9; 2 Tim. 2:11–13; Titus 3:4–8), and Jude's exhortation to contend for the faith once delivered to the saints (Jude 3).[3] Each of these texts captures the idea that God expects his people to take his authoritative revelation, reflect on and study it, restate it in their own words, and pass it down to future generations. The Bible mandates the creation and maintenance of a biblically faithful confessional and catechetical tradition. After surveying the eight texts, the chapter presents an analysis, exploring how the Bible warrants confessions and catechesis, provides protections against dead confessionalism, and reveals an indissoluble link between confession and piety. It then concludes with summary observations about the need for biblically faithful confessions of faith.

1. Mark A. Noll, *A History of Christianity in the United States and Canada* (Grand Rapids: Eerdmans, 2003), 151–52.

2. Noll, *History of Christianity*, 152–53.

3. For other biblical arguments, see Carl R. Trueman, *The Creedal Imperative* (Wheaton: Crossway, 2012), 51–80.

Instruct Future Generations (Exod. 13:14–15)

God's revelation comes in several different forms, but it is more than a divine memorial, an echo of God's voice. Israel is supposed to record God's Word and reflect on it for generations to come. The first time God commands Israel to perform this catechetical task is when he gives instructions for the celebration of the Passover. The Israelites are supposed to reenact, remember, and rationalize the Passover:[4]

> And when in time to come your son asks you, "What does this mean?" you shall say to him, "By a strong hand the LORD brought us out of Egypt, from the house of slavery. For when Pharaoh stubbornly refused to let us go, the LORD killed all the firstborn in the land of Egypt, both the firstborn of man and the firstborn of animals. Therefore I sacrifice to the LORD all the males that first open the womb, but all the firstborn of my sons I redeem." (Exod. 13:14–15)

As Israelite families gathered and partook of the Passover meal, God knew that younger members of the community would ask about its significance. As children tasted the food and stepped into Israel's past, their parents would explain the Passover to them. They would recall God's mighty deliverance from a powerful foe and the judgment that fell upon the firstborn of Egypt, which constituted the rationale for the sacrifice or dedication of the firstborn. This is evident by the use of a result clause: "Therefore [עַל־כֵּן] I sacrifice." The Bible presents a pattern of God's word-act-word revelation along with the subsequent, biblically governed reflection on it and repetition and explanation of it.[5] In other words, God first gave his word to depart Egypt. He then performed a mighty act in delivering Israel from Egypt. God then gave a subsequent word explaining the significance of the act of deliverance. Through God's word-act-word revelation,

---

4. Umberto Cassuto, *A Commentary on the Book of Exodus* (Jerusalem: Magnes, 1997), 140–41; John I. Durham, *Exodus*, WBC 3 (Waco: Word, 1987), 179–80; Peter Enns, *Exodus*, NIVAC (Grand Rapids: Zondervan, 2000), 264; Trueman, *Creedal Imperative*, 58.

5. Geerhardus Vos, "The Idea of Biblical Theology as a Science and as a Theological Discipline," in *Redemptive History and Biblical Interpretation: The Shorter Writings of Geerhardus Vos*, ed. Richard B. Gaffin Jr. (Phillipsburg, NJ: Presbyterian and Reformed, 1980), 3–24.

he is his own interpreter. This same pattern unfolds in the celebration of the Passover. God instructs Israel to perform the Passover. The Israelites perform the act and reflect upon God's word and deliverance. Parents then explain the significance of the Passover to their children with a subsequent word. The revelation-reflection-repetition pattern appears in Jewish halakah, the laws derived from the written and oral forms of the Torah and that extend into the Hellenistic traditions and rituals in Talmudic form.[6] In short, God instructed the Israelites to pass the knowledge and significance of his word-act-word revelation down to future generations. This is a divinely commanded *traditio*. The word *traditio* is derived from the Latin term *trado* (to hand over); hence, a *traditio*—or "tradition"—is a teaching, doctrine, or saying handed down from generation to generation.[7]

Hear O Israel (Deut. 6:4–6)

Many are familiar with the first and greatest commandment, otherwise known as Israel's Shema: "Hear, O Israel: The LORD our God, the LORD is one. You shall love the LORD your God with all your heart and with all your soul and with all your might. And these words that I command you today shall be on your heart" (Deut. 6:4–6). But what might not immediately strike the reader is that this is a confession of Israel's faith for every individual and ultimately the entire nation. The Shema is Israel's fundamental dogma, her magna carta.[8] To preserve Israel's faith, God bound covenant, confession, and catechesis together in the Shema.[9] At the heart of the covenant lies Israel's chief confession of faith, which consists of four words in the Hebrew text: יְהוָה אֱלֹהֵינוּ

---

6. Brevard S. Childs, *The Book of Exodus: A Critical, Theological Commentary* (Louisville: Westminster John Knox, 1974), 207.

7. *Oxford Latin Dictionary*, 2nd ed., vol. 2 (Oxford: Oxford University Press, 2012), s.v. *traditio*; see also Richard A. Muller, *Dictionary of Latin and Greek Theological Terms: Drawn Principally from Protestant Scholastic Theology*, 2nd ed. (Grand Rapids: Baker Academic, 2017), s.v. *traditio*.

8. Peter C. Craigie, *The Book of Deuteronomy*, NICOT (Grand Rapids: Eerdmans, 1976), 169; Daniel I. Block, *How I Love Your Torah, O Lord! Studies in the Book of Deuteronomy* (Eugene, OR: Cascade Books, 2011), 32.

9. J. A. Thompson, *Deuteronomy*, TOTC (Downers Grove, IL: InterVarsity, 1974), 121.

יְהוָה | אֶחָד ("The Lord our God, the Lord is one," Deut. 6:4). Pious Jews recited this confession as a daily prayer, along with Deuteronomy 11:18–32 and Numbers 15:37–41. These references direct the Israelites to bind God's laws on their foreheads, which they took literally and thus tied phylacteries to their heads (i.e., small leather pouches containing miniscule scrolls inscribed with God's commands).[10] The command to bind God's law on their hands, foreheads, doorposts, and gates (Deut. 6:8) was an exhortation to meditate on and to memorize God's law, not to tie leather pouches to their foreheads (see Prov. 6:20–22).[11] Nevertheless, the point of the confession was to cement Israel's collective conviction that Yahweh was to be the sole object of their adoration, affection, and allegiance. Israel's external profession of this brief confession was supposed to serve as the sign of the internal disposition of the heart—the outward confession mirroring the inward conviction. There was no place for prevarication; a disjunction between confession and conviction was inconceivable.[12]

God wanted Israel to profess their faith, and he wanted their profession to protect theological orthodoxy, to express love for God, and to ground catechesis. Israel's confession was a theological guardrail to keep them on the road of biblical monotheism.[13] The confession reminded Israel to be devoted exclusively to Yahweh—confessional and theological orthodoxy going hand in hand with orthopraxy. One cannot take the confession of the Shema on one's lips and then bow down and worship an idol. At the same time, God intended that love would mark this confessional orthodoxy and orthopraxy. Confession of the one true living God was not supposed to spring from legalism, from duty, but rather from love for him. Israel's love for God was to be holistic and total, which Deuteronomy 6:5 captures with the injunction to "love the Lord your God with all your heart and with all your soul and with all your might."[14] According to Hebrew thought,

---

10. Thompson, *Deuteronomy*, 121.
11. Patrick D. Miller, *Deuteronomy*, Interpretation (Louisville: Westminster John Knox, 1990), 105.
12. Thompson, *Deuteronomy*, 121; J. G. McConville, *Deuteronomy*, Apollos Old Testament Commentary (Downers Grove, IL: IVP Academic, 2002), 142.
13. Thompson, *Deuteronomy*, 122.
14. This is a major theme in the book of Deuteronomy. See 4:29; 10:12; 11:13; 13:3; 26:16; 30:2, 6, 10.

the *heart* is the seat of the mind, will, and affections; the *soul* is the source of life and vitality—essentially, one's existence. Deuteronomy 6:5 connecting heart and soul shows that the confession is meant to express whole-person devotion, and the inclusion of one's whole "might" then emphasizes this intention. The New Testament adds another element: the mind (Mark 12:30; Luke 10:27).[15] This love for God, therefore, is not to be merely affective; it is also to consist of obedience and use of the intellect.

As with the divine instructions regarding Passover, God commands Israel to use this confession for catechesis: "And these words that I command you today shall be on your heart. You shall teach them diligently to your children, and shall talk of them when you sit in your house, and when you walk by the way, and when you lie down, and when you rise. You shall bind them as a sign on your hand, and they shall be as frontlets between your eyes. You shall write them on the doorposts of your house and on your gates" (Deut. 6:6–9). Individual Israelites would internalize the significance of this confession through meditation and study. But this internal reflection on the confession would ideally lead to catechesis: instruction of one's family.[16] God intends confession and catechesis to permeate every sphere of life, which is evident in the placement of the Shema (it serves as a spring-board to chapters 12–26).[17] Covenant, love, obedience, and catechesis are all enshrined in confession in this well-known passage from the Old Testament. This confession is a guardian, or a plumb line, to ensure Israel's fidelity to its covenant Lord.[18]

Trustworthy Sayings (1 Tim. 1:15; 3:1; 4:7–9; 2 Tim. 2:11–13; Titus 3:4–8)

The foregoing confessional and catechetical instruction lies at the foundation of Israel's theology; therefore, it should not surprise us

---

15. See Thompson, *Deuteronomy*, 122; McConville, *Deuteronomy*, 142; Miller, *Deuteronomy*, 102–3.

16. See Deut. 4:9; 6:20–25; 11:19.

17. Craigie, *Deuteronomy*, 170; Miller, *Deuteronomy*, 97.

18. William L. Moran, "The Ancient Near Eastern Background of the Love of God in Deuteronomy," *CBQ* 25, no. 1 (1963): 77–87; Miller, *Deuteronomy*, 98.

to find the same pattern in the New Testament. This pattern appears prominently in Paul's Pastoral Epistles and his five trustworthy sayings (πιστὸς ὁ λόγος).[19] What does the apostle intend to convey by this lexeme, and what are its origins? The most plausible idea is that these are objective restatements of what Jesus taught about himself, as recorded in the Gospels, and also reiterations of other biblical teachings. That is, they repeat phrases and concepts that appear in the Gospels or in other portions of Scripture.[20] Paul often employs earlier catechetical or liturgical material.[21] The formula itself, "this is a trustworthy saying," echoes the commendation following the Shema.[22] In other words, Paul uses the same catechetical and covenantal pattern established in the Passover and the Shema.

In the first of Paul's statements, he writes, "The saying is trustworthy and deserving of full acceptance, that Christ Jesus came into the world to save sinners, of whom I am the foremost" (1 Tim. 1:15). This idea is prominent in all four of the Gospels.[23] Paul makes this brief objective statement based on Christ's self-testimony to demonstrate that the Savior's teaching has come to fruition in his own life and in the lives of all those who respond to Christ in faith.[24] Here Paul reiterates divine revelation in his letters—restating Christ's teaching for the purpose of instructing the church. In this particular case, Paul reiterates Christ's teaching under the superintendence and inspiration of the Holy Spirit (though we will see that Paul records an uninspired version of this practice when he addresses the church's doctrinal reflections on revelation in his letters). The other instances

19. For an overview of the origins and use of the formula, see I. Howard Marshall, *The Pastoral Epistles*, ICC (London: T&T Clark, 1999), 326–30; George W. Knight III, *The Faithful Sayings in the Pastoral Letters* (Grand Rapids: Baker, 1979); R. Alastair Campbell, "Identifying the Faithful Sayings in the Pastoral Epistles," *JSNT* 16, no. 54 (October 1994): 73–86; José M. Bover, "Fidelis Sermo," *Biblica* 19, no. 11 (1938): 74–79; W. A. Oldfather and L. W. Daly, "A Quotation from Menander in the Pastoral Epistles?" *Classical Philology* 38, no. 3 (1943): 202–4.

20. George W. Knight III, *The Pastoral Epistles: A Commentary on the Greek Text*, NIGTC (Grand Rapids: Eerdmans, 1992), 101–2.

21. Marshall, *Pastoral Epistles*, 328.

22. J. N. D. Kelly, *The Pastoral Epistles*, BNTC (Peabody, MA: Hendrickson, 1998), 54.

23. See Matt. 9:13; Mark 2:17; Luke 5:32; 19:10; John 12:46–47; 16:28; 18:37.

24. Knight, *Pastoral Letters*, 101–2.

of Paul's "trustworthy saying" formula reveal the range of topics that fall under this scriptural rubric.

In the second saying, Paul writes, "The saying is trustworthy: If anyone aspires to the office of overseer, he desires a noble task" (1 Tim. 3:1). Why would he identify this statement about aspiring to the office of overseer as a trustworthy saying? Paul was generally concerned to establish order in the churches that he pastored. This is why Paul, for example, left Titus in Crete: so that he "might put what remained into order, and appoint elders in every town" (Titus 1:5). In this case, Paul's trustworthy saying reflects the apostles' lively and deep interest in church order, demonstrated in 1 Timothy 3 and other places in the New Testament.[25] This New Testament ecclesiastical order reflects Old Testament Israel's interest in the same topic (e.g., Exod. 18:13–27). Beyond the scope of church order, the other reason Paul commends this statement is that the desire to serve as an overseer is "noble" (καλοῦ ἔργου)—literally, "a good work."[26]

The third occurrence of the trustworthy saying formula follows Paul's statement about the importance of training in godliness: "Have nothing to do with irreverent, silly myths. Rather train yourself for godliness; for while bodily training is of some value, godliness is of value in every way, as it holds promise for the present life and also for the life to come. The saying is trustworthy and deserving of full acceptance" (1 Tim. 4:7–9). This particular testimony finds precedent in Christ's teaching in Luke 18:29–30: "Truly, I say to you, there is no one who has left house or wife or brothers or parents or children, for the sake of the kingdom of God, who will not receive many times more in this time, and in the age to come eternal life." First Timothy 4:8b echoes Christ's words recorded in the Gospel that there is great reward for those who renounce everything for his sake. The early church took this dominical teaching, generalized it, and produced a trustworthy saying about godliness.[27]

---

25. Knight, *Pastoral Letters*, 153; Kelly, *Pastoral Epistles*, 72–73; cf. Bruce J. Malina and John J. Pilch, *Social-Science Commentary on the Deutero-Pauline Letters* (Minneapolis: Fortress, 2013), 117. See Acts 6:1–6; 14:21–23; 20:17–35; Rom. 12:6–8; 1 Cor. 12:28; Phil. 1:1; 1 Thess. 5:12–22; 1 Tim. 5:17–23; Titus 1:5–9; Heb. 12:7; 1 Pet. 5:1–4.

26. Knight, *Pastoral Letters*, 154–55.

27. Knight, *Pastoral Letters*, 201.

The fourth trustworthy saying appears in 2 Timothy 2:11–13, where Paul writes:

> The saying is trustworthy, for:
>
>> If we have died with him, we will also live with him;
>> if we endure, we will also reign with him;
>> if we deny him, he also will deny us;
>> if we are faithless, he remains faithful—
>
> for he cannot deny himself.

This trustworthy saying finds its conceptual roots in Christ's teaching: "You will be hated by all for my name's sake. But the one who endures to the end will be saved" (Matt. 10:22).[28] But beyond Christ's teaching, the other source of the saying might be the church at Rome and their reflection on Paul's letter to them, specifically the sixth chapter: "Now if we have died with Christ, we believe that we will also live with him" (Rom. 6:8). In other words, Paul draws from the church's reflection on his teaching—that is, he draws from church tradition.[29] This does not mean that Paul recognizes the authority of church tradition as having precedence over Scripture; rather, it means he recognizes that the church can accurately proclaim again the truth of authoritative revelation in its own words. In short, the one who professes faith in Christ is in union with him and shares in his sufferings in the Christian life. But through these sufferings Paul exhorts Timothy to persevere and assures him of Christ's faithfulness to the redeemed.[30]

The fifth trustworthy saying appears in Titus 3:4–8, where Paul reflects on the free nature of redemption:

> But when the goodness and loving kindness of God our Savior appeared, he saved us, not because of works done by us in righteousness, but according to his own mercy, by the washing of regeneration and

28. Knight, *Pastoral Letters*, 404–5. See also Matt. 24:13; Mark 13:13.
29. Malina and Pilch, *Deutero-Pauline Letters*, 151; Kelly, *Pastoral Epistles*, 179; Marshall, *Pastoral Epistles*, 739.
30. Knight, *Pastoral Letters*, 407–8.

renewal of the Holy Spirit, whom he poured out on us richly through Jesus Christ our Savior, so that being justified by his grace we might become heirs according to the hope of eternal life. The saying is trustworthy, and I want you to insist on these things, so that those who have believed in God may be careful to devote themselves to good works. (Titus 3:4–8)

Commentators suggest that this trustworthy saying was likely a terse creedal-liturgical statement that would have been used in a baptismal setting, or perhaps it was part of a baptismal hymn.[31] The fact that the saying is trinitarian—like the baptismal formula of the Great Commission (Matt. 28:18–19)—points in this direction.[32] By describing verses 4–7 as a trustworthy saying, Paul "certifies that he has faithfully handed down the tradition he received."[33] But Paul, importantly, identifies the saying about the redemptive work of the triune God as an impelling factor in the pursuit of good works: "The saying is trustworthy, and I want you to insist on these things, so that [ἵνα] those who have believed in God may be careful to devote themselves to good works" (Titus 3:8). The result clause indicates that the trustworthy saying and the truth it contains motivate believers to do good works.

These five trustworthy sayings cover a range of topics, including redemption, church order, and ethical conduct. But the fundamental principle that underlies them all is that the church appropriated scriptural revelation, restated it in its own terms, and promulgated it within the church. In these five instances, under divine inspiration, Paul incorporated these digested forms of revelation into his own letters, thereby confirming the sayings' veracity and consonance with earlier revelation. With the closing of the canon and the cessation of new revelation, the revelation-reflection-repetition loop no longer exists. Nevertheless, the fact that the revelation-confession pattern has precedents both in the Old Testament and in the New confirms that, with appropriate scriptural safeguards, there is biblical warrant for the church to create and maintain confessions of faith.

31. Malina and Pilch, *Deutero-Pauline Letters*, 89.
32. Knight, *Pastoral Letters*, 350.
33. Malina and Pilch, *Deutero-Pauline Letters*, 90.

The Faith Once Delivered (Jude 3)

One of the chief concerns of Jude's epistle is to address and refute false teachers. Jude writes, "For certain people have crept in unnoticed who long ago were designated for this condemnation, ungodly people, who pervert the grace of our God into sensuality and deny our only Master and Lord, Jesus Christ" (Jude 4). In contrast to the false teachers—who pervert the grace of God and thus, ultimately, God's teaching contained in divine revelation—Jude exhorts his recipients to "contend for the faith that was once for all delivered to the saints" (Jude 3). Jude seeks to distinguish orthodoxy from heterodoxy, and so he refers to "the faith"—that is, the content of what the church is supposed to believe. In other words, he refers to *fides quae creditur* (the faith that is believed), the content of faith, rather than to *fides qua creditur* (the faith by which [it] is believed), that is, the faith of the believer.[34] This idea is common in the New Testament, such as when Paul states, "They only were hearing it said, 'He who used to persecute us is now preaching the faith he once tried to destroy'" (Gal. 1:23). "The faith" is another way to refer to the message of the gospel.[35] This means that Paul and Jude believe there is an objective message to which the church needs to adhere, a faith that is different from the body of opinions promoted by the false teachers.

Jude writes to his recipients that God has delivered this faith, an objective body of knowledge, to the saints (i.e., to the church). As with the Passover liturgy, through which parents instruct their children and hand over the knowledge of God's saving work from generation to generation, God has "handed over" (παραδοθείσῃ) the faith to the saints. This is, in fact, how theologians translated this term from Greek into Latin: "*Pro fide quae semel tradita est sanctis*" (The faith that was once delivered to the saints).[36] This faith was not discovered by the saints; it was given to them by

---

34. Richard J. Bauckham, *Jude, 2 Peter*, WBC 50 (Waco: Word, 1983), 32; Muller, *Dictionary*, s.vv. *fides qua creditur*, *fides quae creditur*.

35. Bauckham, *Jude, 2 Peter*, 32.

36. Herman Witsius, *Meletemata Leidensia: Quibus Continentur Praelectiones de Vita et Rebus Gestis Pauli Apostoli. Nec Non Dissertationum Exegeticarum Duodecas. Denique Commentarius in Epistolam Judae Apostoli* (Leiden, 1703), 463.

God.[37] The chain of communication goes from God to the apostles and then, finally, to the saints (τοῖς ἁγίοις). With talk of the faith being "delivered" or "handed over" (παραδοθείσῃ), Jude echoes the Jewish tradition (παράδωσις) terminology, which encapsulates the practice of the transmission of an authoritative tradition.[38] This revelatory tradition is fixed and unchanging, as is evident by Jude's use of the phrase "once for all" (ἅπαξ).[39] The fact that he contrasts the objective faith once delivered to the saints with the erroneous doctrine and ethics of the false teachers indicates that Jude upholds the connection between orthodoxy and orthopraxy, between doctrine and ethics. His concern is that the saints adhere to the common, objective faith and salvation (κοινῆς ἡμῶν σωτηρίας) handed down to them and to ensure that their ethical conduct does not go astray.[40] Jude presents the idea that the Scriptures contain a deposit of truth that the church has to pass down and guard from generation to generation.[41] In Jude's words, the church is supposed to "contend for the faith once delivered."

Analysis

The foregoing eight passages from the Old and New Testaments demonstrate how integral confession and catechism are to the covenant people of God. The Bible itself provides confessions of faith, such as the Shema, and commands the people of God to embrace them and to inculcate children and converts with their teachings through catechesis, thereby growing the covenant community. Such an ethos does not rest on the mere repetition of biblical formulae but

37. Thomas Manton, *A Practical Commentary, or An Exposition with Notes on the Epistle of Jude* (London, 1658), 143, 146–47.
38. See Col. 2:6–8; 2 Thess. 3:6. Also note the similar idea in 2 Cor. 11:3–4; Gal. 1:8–9.
39. Bauckham, *Jude, 2 Peter*, 33–34; Oscar Cullman, *The Early Church* (Philadelphia: Westminster, 1956), 59–99, esp. 63; Manton, *Jude*, 154–55.
40. See David Dickson, *An Exposition of All of St. Paul's Epistles Together with An Explanation of Those Other Epistles of the Apostles, St. James, Peter, John & Jude* (London, 1659), 320; Manton, *Jude*, 137–43; Witsius, *Meletemata Leidensia*, 462. Cf. Bauckham, *Jude, 2 Peter*, 34.
41. Manton, *Jude*, 152–53.

requires explanation and interpretation. Regarding this expansive reiteration of biblical teaching, we should note three things: (1) the biblical warrant for, and necessity of, confessions and catechesis; (2) the biblical protections against dead traditionalism; and (3) the relationship between confession and piety.

1. The Biblical Warrant for, and Necessity of, Confessions and Catechesis

Biblical confessions run in two directions. They look back at God's past redemptive activity and revelation, erecting ebenezers to remind the church of what he has done. And they lean forward into the future, as parents are to educate their children in the meaning of the Passover, and as Paul draws Timothy's attention to trustworthy sayings that, while having originated in the past, are yet supposed to echo into the future in the lives of those who embrace them. As the saints to whom Jude writes recall the faith once delivered, they are supposed to preserve it for the present and the future. The traditions that the biblical authors passed on to future generations were the living faith of the dead, not traditionalism's dead faith of the living.[42] In the words of Johann Wolfgang von Goethe (1749–1832), "What you have as heritage, Take now as task; For thus you will make it your own."[43] In other words, each generation receives the confessional tradition through catechesis and appropriates it for themselves. One cannot give away what one does not own; thus, each generation must own the truths that the confessions of the Scriptures teach.

But in the appropriation of biblical truth, one must distinguish between the inspired and inerrant teaching of Scripture and its subsequent, uninspired explanations and interpretations. God explains the significance of the Passover and tells parents what to say to their children about it (Exod. 13:14–16). But surely the children's questions will go beyond the divinely given catechetical answer, which

---

42. Jaroslav Pelikan, *The Vindication of Tradition* (New Haven: Yale University Press, 1984), 43.
43. As quoted in Pelikan, *Vindication of Tradition*, 82; see also in Johann Wolfgang von Goethe, *Faust*, trans. Walter Kaufmann (New York: Anchor Books, 1990), lines 683–89, pp. 114–15.

means that parents will have to interpret the event and its divinely revealed explanation to provide relevant answers. This pattern unfolds in Paul's "trustworthy sayings." These sayings have no direct precedent. They are not quotations from earlier revelation but summary restatements of biblical truths. These sayings show that the church, from the very beginning, has reflected on biblical revelation, interpreted it, and restated it in its own words. These particular sayings were so consonant with biblical revelation that the apostle Paul incorporated them into his divinely inspired letters to Timothy and Titus. Nevertheless, the existence of the trustworthy sayings proves that there is a legitimate place for a scripturally subordinated confessional tradition.

This conclusion should not surprise us. It follows the same well-worn path as several other ecclesiastical practices, such as prayer and preaching. God does not restrict the saints solely to repeating the words of Scripture in their prayers. To be sure, Christ provides a model prayer (Matt. 6:9–13), but it serves as a guide, not as a prescription. When Christians pray, their words must conform to the teaching of Scripture. But life, circumstance, and desire typically—and appropriately—shape the content of prayer. The same pattern appears in preaching. God does not tell preachers merely to open the Bible, read it, and then close it. That would not be preaching; it would be reading the Word—which is certainly a necessary part of worship, but it is not the only part. Preachers are supposed to read the Word, reflect on it, interpret it, and demonstrate how it relates to the life of the church. The book of Nehemiah captures this practice: "They read from the book, from the Law of God, clearly, and they gave the sense, so that the people understood the reading" (Neh. 8:8).

In the same vein, then, the Scriptures instruct the church to take the Bible's teaching and to study, comprehend, and proclaim it again in their own words for both catechesis and defense of the faith. The existence of the "trustworthy sayings" demonstrates that the apostolic church was doing this very thing and that their confessions existed in oracular form. That Paul documented these maxims also shows that the church can and should record in writing their own trustworthy sayings. They serve both to catechize the church and to defend it against the deception of false teachers. For this task, Christ has given the church the gift of teachers. As Thomas Manton (1620–77) observes, Christ has given "*Prophets* and *Apostles* to the Church to *write Scripture*, hath also given *Pastors* and *Teachers* to *open* and *apply* Scripture, that so still it might be *delivered* to the Saints, and also to *vindicate* the doctrine of it when *opposed*."[44] In every age, light arises to oppose darkness; every time false teachers try to introduce the poison of false doctrine, Christ sends good teachers with an antidote. Athanasius (ca. 296–373), for example, opposed Arius (ca. 250–ca. 336), Augustine (354–430) combatted Pelagius (d. ca. 418), Martin Luther (1483–1546) stood against Rome, and J. Gresham Machen (1881–1937) fought against modernism. The church has never lacked good teachers. Manton encourages his readers: "Look as in War, as the *Arts of Battery* and *methods of destruction* do increase, so also doth skill in *Fortification*; and in the Church God still bestoweth gifts for the further explication of Truth."[45]

Historic confessions are one way that the church can consult the wisdom of its luminaries from the past and benefit from Christ's gifts to the church throughout the ages. In short, the Bible mandates the creation and promulgation of a biblically subordinated tradition for the edification of the church and the defense of the faith.

2. The Biblical Protections against Dead Traditionalism

But just because the Bible enjoins confessionalism for the well-being of the church does not mean that there are no potential dangers. Confessions embody tradition—they enshrine and hand down what the church at a particular point in history believes and professes. The Bible, therefore, commends the creation of a biblically subordinated tradition; at the same time, the danger of severing tradition from the Bible always lies close at hand. For example, Christ and his disciples ran up against the "tradition of the elders," which was given precedence over the commandments of God (Matt. 15:2–3). For the sake of the preservation of their tradition, the religious leaders nullified the law of God (Matt. 15:6). To be sure, Paul inveighs against "human traditions," those that seek to displace the Word

---

44. Manton, *Jude*, 150.
45. Manton, *Jude*, 150.

of God (Gal. 1:14; Col. 2:8). But he commends biblically faithful traditions. He exhorts the Corinthians to maintain the traditions he gave to them (1 Cor. 11:2). Likewise, speaking to the Thessalonians, he says, "Stand firm and hold to the traditions that you were taught by us, either by our spoken word or by our letter" (2 Thess. 2:15).[46] Confessional abuse does not negate the necessity of creating and maintaining a doctrinal tradition through confessions. One must always subordinate the church's confessions to the Scriptures. The Bereans went to Scripture to verify Paul's teaching, to ensure his fidelity to divine revelation (Acts 17:11). And Paul, famously, opposed Peter when Peter transgressed the boundaries of orthodoxy (Gal. 2:11). But just because the church might fall into error does not negate the importance and necessity of creating and preserving doctrinal tradition through confessions.

3. The Relationship between Confession and Piety

One of the common criticisms of confessionalism is that it produces a dry and dusty orthodoxy devoid of piety. But the Bible shows that, ideally, there is supposed to be an irrefragable connection between confession and piety. Biblically faithful confessions are part of a vibrant corporate and individual faith that yields the fruit of piety in practice. When God instructs the Israelites to catechize their children, it is so that future generations will continue in their faith and in their devotion to their covenant Lord. Jude exhorts his recipients to contend for the faith once delivered to the saints, the deposit of truth, to ensure that false teachers cannot secure a beachhead from which to invade the church. But Jude's concern is not merely to preserve a body of truth for intellectual musing but to ensure that this doctrine informs the piety and practice of the church; the false teachers, recall, "pervert the grace of our God into sensuality" (Jude 4). Similarly, Paul's trustworthy sayings address matters such as church order, and he demonstrates the link between confession and piety when he writes, "The saying is trustworthy, and I want you to insist on these things, so that those who have believed in God may be careful to devote themselves to good works" (Titus 3:8).

46. See also 2 Thess. 3:6.

But love for God is among the chief fruits of a vibrant confessionalism. Love lies at the heart of the Shema; covenant is a bond that provides the context for its participants to love one another. God showers Israel with his love, and, conversely, the Israelites are supposed to reciprocate by showing their love through obedience. Covenant and confession go hand in hand: God, in love, establishing the covenant with Israel and Israel confessing the faith once delivered to the saints, the holy tradition handed down from generation to generation. The people of God show their love as they confess the doctrines of the Bible and as those truths inform their conduct, all to the glory and love of God. The Shema is at the same time a doctrinal confession, a guardrail to keep Israel on the road of covenant fidelity, a textbook for instructing future generations, and a powerful poetic idiom with which to express heartfelt love for God. Far from a cold, rationalistic account of the faith, the Bible identifies confession as a vital ligament and cord of love connecting the church to its faithful covenant Lord. Historic confessions also inform and animate the church's worship.

Conclusion

The Bible not only expects but also arguably mandates that the people of God reflect upon and restate biblical teaching faithfully in their own words. As popular as the "no creed but the Bible" confession might be (and it is itself a confession—a brief one, but a confession nonetheless), the Bible calls the church to a deeper contemplation on the truths that it teaches. Pastors must be prepared to explain the meaning of Scripture and of the rites of the church; parents must be prepared to answer questions from their children. And all Christians must contend for the faith once delivered to the saints. In this engagement with the Bible's teachings, Christians cannot merely repeat a cento of biblical statements but must explain, interpret, and restate in their own words what the Bible means. But we theological hobbits are not the first ones to encounter the Bible. We must stand on the shoulders of giants to catch a glimpse of the glory of our triune God. That is, we must benefit from Christ's gifts to the church and glean knowledge from the *traditio*, the prayerful meditations and doctrinal conclusions of our great ancestors in the faith. We must always check their work against the supreme authority in doctrine and life, the Holy Scriptures. Nevertheless, as we join hands with our ancestors, we can create trustworthy sayings about our common salvation and look to the horizon as we catechize future generations so that they too may contend for the faith once delivered to the saints. Far from being unbiblical, confessions of faith are employed by the Scriptures themselves and are necessary for the well-being of the church.

TWO

Reformed Confessions (1500–1700)

Introduction

Nineteenth-century Scottish theologian Horatius Bonar perceived a disadvantageous shift in the confessions of the seventeenth century:

It may be questioned whether the Church gained anything by the exchange of the Reformation standards for those of the seventeenth century. The scholastic mould in which the latter are cast has somewhat trenched upon the ease and breadth which mark the former; and the skillful metaphysics employed at Westminster in giving lawyer-like precision to each statement, have imparted a local and temporary aspect to the new which did not belong to the more ancient standards.[1]

Bonar believed that the simpler formulations of the Reformation were more likely to stand the test of time rather than, what was in his mind, the dated "theology of the covenant." He believed that the Reformation confessions employed biblical language, whereas the Westminster Confession employed scholastic language. The

1. Horatius Bonar, *Catechisms of the Scottish Reformation* (London, 1866), viii.

19

Reformation embodied "doctrine, life, action, nobly blended." But seventeenth-century theologians did not preserve the balance because "the purely dogmatical preponderated."[2]

Bonar expressed his preference for the Reformation-era confessions and catechisms over and against those of the seventeenth century, a preference that persists in the analyses of T. F. Torrance (1913–2007), John Murray (1898–1975), and John Frame (1939–).[3] According to Frame, for example, Reformation theology is personal and existential, whereas seventeenth-century scholastic theology is more detailed, argumentative, and "academically respectable." Frame suggests that scholastic theology was responsible for the church's decline into liberalism.[4] John Calvin (1509–64) and Martin Luther (1483–1546) supposedly taught a theology that made no concessions to Greek philosophy and set forth a purely biblical metaphysic, epistemology, and ethic.[5] Calvin captured this theology, which was the basis of all Reformed doctrine, in his *Institutes*.[6] The implication is that seventeenth-century theology, with its more academically minded scholastic confessions and catechisms, represents a devolution of the purely biblical Reformation theology. As common as this narrative is, it represents a misunderstanding of the historical evidence and the relationship between the Reformation and post-Reformation eras.

Rather than pit the Reformation era against the post-Reformation era, this chapter defends the thesis that the confessions of both have a legitimate organic link. The post-Reformation confessions and catechisms are a necessary development and outgrowth of the Reformation.[7] This is not to say that the confessions of both periods are identical; there are certainly differences. But the variations between

---

2. Bonar, *Catechisms*, viii–ix.
3. T. F. Torrance, *The School of Faith: The Catechisms of the Reformed Church* (1959; repr., Eugene, OR: Wipf & Stock, 1996), xvii; John Murray, "Covenant Theology," in *Collected Writings of John Murray*, vol. 4, *Studies in Theology* (Edinburgh: Banner of Truth, 1982), 216–40, esp. 217–22; John Frame, *A History of Western Philosophy and Theology* (Phillipsburg, NJ: P&R, 2015), 175.
4. Frame, *History of Western Philosophy*, 175.
5. Frame, *History of Western Philosophy*, 206.
6. Frame, *History of Western Philosophy*, 212.
7. See Carl R. Trueman, *The Creedal Imperative* (Wheaton: Crossway, 2012), 81–108.

the documents of each period represent not declension or perversion but rather development due to several factors: local issues and controversies, church politics, varied reception of older traditions, responses to newer philosophical approaches, and specific educational concerns.[8] In other words, Reformation and post-Reformation theologians did not write their confessions in a historical vacuum. Personal belief, corporate conviction, and circumstance flow together in the process of writing a confession. Since history and circumstances are not static, one should not expect that confessional expressions spanning several hundred years will all be the same.

To demonstrate the organic unity of Reformation and post-Reformation confessions, this chapter surveys the history of Reformed confessions from 1500–1700 by tracing the major confessional documents of the Reformation (1500–1565), Early Orthodox (1565–ca. 1640), and High Orthodox (ca. 1640–1700) periods. Each section examines key confessions, doctrinal examples, and the historical events surrounding the creation of the confessions in order to draw an accurate comparison between the Reformation and post-Reformation confessions. It will become clear that the post-Reformation confessions— including the Canons of Dort (1619), the Westminster Standards (1648), the Savoy Declaration (1658), and the Second London Confession (1689)—represent not a devolution of Reformation theology but rather its natural, and faithful, development.

Reformation (1500–1565)

The Protestant Reformation was a movement that began with individual theologians questioning the authority of the church on various theological issues. In popular lore, Luther started the Reformation on October 31, 1517, when he nailed his Ninety-Five Theses to the castle door at Wittenberg. But in 1517, Luther was still very much entrenched in the theology of the day, and it would take a number of years before Luther the Reformer was born. As the reform movement

8. Richard A. Muller, "Reformed Theology Between 1600–1800," in *The Oxford Handbook of Early Modern Theology, 1600–1800*, ed. Ulrich L. Lehner, Richard A. Muller, and A. G. Roeber (Oxford: Oxford University Press, 2016), 167.

grew, there were two chief issues that faced the Holy Roman Empire: (1) repelling Turkish armies, which had besieged Vienna in the fall of 1529 and still held significant sections of Hungary, and (2) addressing the religious tensions within the Empire.[9] Emperor Charles V (1500–1558) called an imperial diet in June of 1530 and asked theological protagonists to present representative statements of faith. Luther was unable to attend the diet but sent Philipp Melanchthon (1497–1560), who for the occasion drafted the Augsburg Confession in consultation with Luther; this confession was based on two earlier documents, the Schwabach Articles (1529) and the Torgau Articles (1530). Martin Bucer (1491–1551) was part of a group of theologians that presented the Tetrapolitan Confession on behalf of Strasbourg, Memmingen, Lindau, and Constance. Ulrich Zwingli (1484–1531) wrote and presented his personal confession, *Ratio Fidei* (Account of Faith). And Roman Catholic officials delivered a refutation of the Augsburg Confession: the Papal Confutation, which elicited a rejoinder from Melanchthon in the form of his Apology (1531).[10] This historical context shaped the nature of these initial Reformation confessions.

Each of these confessions was written very quickly by an individual or a small group (as in the case of the Tetrapolitan Confession) for the purpose of politically and theologically legitimizing the nascent Protestant movement. The speed with which these confessions were written undoubtedly played a role in their shape; moreover, their purpose also pushed the documents in a certain direction. The authors focused on issues that divided Protestant conviction from Roman Catholic. The Augsburg, Tetrapolitan, and Zwinglian confessions do not have formal articles on the doctrine of Scripture; the Tetrapolitan has a chapter on the "subject-matter of sermons" (1), but this arguably has more to do with the theology of preaching than with the doctrine of Scripture per se. This is not to say that Protestant

---

9. Charlotte Methuen, "Luther's Life," in *The Oxford Handbook of Martin Luther's Theology*, ed. Robert Kolb, Irene Dingel, and L'Ubomír Batka (Oxford: Oxford University Press, 2014), 23.

10. Methuen, "Luther's Life," 23; Jaroslav Pelikan and Valerie Hotchkiss, eds., *Creeds and Confessions of the Faith in the Christian Tradition*, 4 vols. (New Haven: Yale University Press, 2003), 2:49. Unless otherwise noted, all references to confessions and catechisms come from these volumes.

and Roman views of Scripture were in perfect agreement; they were not. But the framers of these confessions believed there were more pressing matters.

The Augsburg Confession begins with God (1) and then treats original sin (2), Christology (3), justification (4), office of the ministry (5), and new obedience (6). This outline quickly shows that the doctrine of justification was central to the debate. The Tetrapolitan Confession, likewise, starts by addressing the proper subject matter for sermons (1) and moves on to discuss Trinity and Christology (2), justification (3), and good works (4). Another intensely debated topic between Protestants and Roman Catholics, as well as between Lutherans and the Reformed, was sacramentology. These confessions were written in the wake of the Marburg Colloquy (1529), where Luther and Zwingli had debated the nature of Christ's presence in the Lord's Supper. These early confessions, therefore, address this topic in great detail. The Augsburg Confession has chapters on the church (7–8), baptism (9), the Lord's Supper (10), confession (11), repentance (12), and the use of the sacraments (13). The Tetrapolitan Confession, similarly, contains chapters on human traditions (14), the church (15), the sacraments (16), baptism (17), the Eucharist (18), and the Mass (19). Fresh off his recent debates with Luther, Zwingli addresses the topics of the church and the sacraments in his *Ratio Fidei* in several long, elaborately written pages (sec. 6–8). Pressing concerns and historical circumstances played a significant role in the creation and shape of these documents.

The same is true for the second wave of Reformed confessions— written, as they were, in the shadow of the Roman Catholic Council of Trent (1545–63). All appearing near the conclusion of the council, the French Confession (1559), Second Helvetic Confession (1566), Belgic Confession (1561), and Heidelberg Catechism (1563) interact with the new Catholic arguments and respond to the council's major doctrinal pronouncements. The Council of Trent met in three distinct periods (1545–49, 1551–52, and 1562–63). During the first period (sessions 1–8), the council issued decrees on faith (sess. 3), Scripture and tradition (sess. 4), original sin (sess. 5), justification and good works (sess. 6), and the sacraments (sess. 7). During the second period (1551–52), it issued a decree on the Eucharist (sess. 13) and condemned all Protestant views on the supper.[11] In the third period the council largely dealt with the sacrifice of the mass (sess. 22), holy orders (sess. 23), marriage (sess. 24), and purgatory (sess. 25).[12] It should come as no surprise, then, that the second-wave Reformed confessions addressed these doctrines in greater detail.

An example of the ongoing polemical dialogue surfaces in Trent's first decree and its definition of the canon: "The council has decided that a written list of the sacred books should be included in this decree in case a doubt should occur to anyone as to which are the books which are accepted by this council."[13] The decree then lists the sixty-six books of what thereafter became the Protestant canon, but it also includes the Apocryphal books of 1 Esdras, Tobit, Judith, Ecclesiasticus, and 1 and 2 Maccabees. Moreover, the council also issued a decree mandating the use of the Vulgate as the only authentic version of the Bible for public readings, debates, sermons, and teaching on doctrine. Naturally, the second-generation Reformed confessions responded in kind. The French Confession presents three articles (3–5) on the doctrine of Scripture, including its own list of canonical books and rejecting the Apocryphal books. The Belgic, which was based in part on the French Confession, has seven articles (1–7) that address the doctrine of Scripture. The Second Helvetic has a chapter on Scripture with nine articles that address the canon, preaching, illumination of the Spirit, and heresies related to the denial of Scripture (1). In another chapter, containing six articles, it explains the relationship between Scripture and tradition (2).

These second-generation documents are formally different but substantively similar to the first-generation Reformation confessions. They do not introduce new doctrines but rather engage Roman Catholic criticisms of Reformation teaching. But three other factors contribute to the ongoing development of Reformed confessions. First, second-generation Reformers were now at the helm. More theologians were contributing to the Reformed confessional tradition. The French Confession, for example, began life as a joint effort of French and Swiss theologians, which was then revised by John Calvin,

11. Pelikan and Hotchkiss, *Creeds*, 2:819–20.
12. Pelikan and Hotchkiss, *Creeds*, 2:861–71.
13. Council of Trent, Session 4, 8 April 1546.

Theodore Beza (1519–1605), and Pierre Viret (1511–71) and finally adopted in revised form by the first French National Synod in 1559. Second, these larger confessions of faith served two purposes: they were doctrinal bulwarks against the claims of Trent, and they were educational instruments. First-generation Reformers launched the Reformation, but second-generation Reformers had to preserve the movement and educate and train new ministers of the gospel.[14] Educational needs were the impulse behind more expansive treatments of doctrine that spanned from God to the eschaton. Alongside these confessional and educational developments were ongoing debates between Reformed and Roman Catholic theologians, fed by doctrinal works such as Calvin's *Institutes* (1559), Melanchthon's *Loci Communes* (in various editions), Heinrich Bullinger's *Decades* (1550), Andreas Hyperius's *Elements of the Christian Religion* (1563), and Wolfgang Musculus's *Common Places* (1560).[15]

Third, the Council of Trent was very specific at times and included common scholastic distinctions to explain their doctrines. In its decree on justification, for example, Trent states that justification involves the infusion of faith, hope, and charity. And the council delineates the causes of justification by means of fourfold Aristotelian causality, a common scholastic distinction: the final cause is the glory of God, the efficient cause is the Holy Spirit, the meritorious cause is the work of Christ, and the instrumental cause is the sacrament of baptism.[16] These conciliar statements raised the debate to a new level. The Tetrapolitan Confession states only that justification is "to be received by faith alone," which is followed by a series of quotations from Scripture (3). The statement is rather untechnical. By way of comparison to the Tetrapolitan Confession's single article on justification, the Second Helvetic presents an entire chapter with six articles. In contrast to Trent's infused righteousness, it specifies that God justifies sinners by the imputed righteousness of Christ: "Properly speaking, therefore, God alone justifies us, and justifies only

---

14. See Amy Nelson Burnett, *Teaching the Reformation: Ministers and Their Message in Basel, 1529–1629* (Oxford: Oxford University Press, 2006), 1–90.

15. Philip Benedict, *Christ's Churches Purely Reformed: A Social History of Calvinism* (New Haven: Yale University Press, 2002), 49–65.

16. Council of Trent, "Decree on Justification," Session 6, 13 January 1547.

on account of Christ, not imputing sins to us but by imputing righteousness to us" (15.3). The Second Helvetic substantively engages the issues raised by Trent regarding the causes of salvation but does not invoke fourfold causality to explain them. Other confessions, however, do echo this scholastic language, as when the Belgic Confession states, "We do not mean, properly speaking, that it is faith itself that justifies us—for faith is only the instrument by which we embrace Christ, our righteousness" (22).

That being said, even though these Reformed confessions do not invoke the same scholastic distinctions as Trent, Reformers such as John Calvin, Zacharias Ursinus (1534–83), and Peter Martyr Vermigli (1499–1562) employed fourfold causality in their own treatments of justification, and especially in their refutations of Tridentine doctrine.[17] In other words, contrary to popular opinion, the Reformers did not eschew all forms of scholasticism. The tools of the scholastic method were never completely absent from Reformed theology.[18] But in spite of their use of scholastic distinctions, second-generation Reformers did not incorporate prominent scholastic elements into their confessions, even when baited by Trent's use of the same. This is because they distinguished between technical theological works and confessions of faith, the latter being corporate documents intended for use by the broadest possible audience, from trained theologians to lay parishioners. Evidence of this conscientious division of labor appears in the warm pastoral tones of the Heidelberg Catechism, which contrast with the more technical elaborations that Ursinus provides in his lectures on the catechism. The general avoidance of scholastic language in the second-generation Reformation-era confessions provides a benchmark against which to compare the post-Reformation-era confessions. In short, there is little difference between the confessions

17. John Calvin, *Canons and Decrees of the Council of Trent, with the Antidote* (1547), in *John Calvin: Tracts and Letters*, ed. Henry Beveridge, 7 vols. (1851; repr., Edinburgh: Banner of Truth, 2009), 3:116; Peter Martyr Vermigli, *The Peter Martyr Library*, trans. and ed. Frank A. James III, vol. 8, *Predestination and Justification: Two Theological Loci* (Kirksville, MO: Thomas Jefferson University Press, 2003), 159; Zacharias Ursinus, *The Commentary of Dr. Zacharias Ursinus on the Heidelberg Catechism* (Phillipsburg, NJ: Presbyterian and Reformed, n.d.), 330–31.

18. See Richard A. Muller, *The Unaccommodated Calvin: Studies in the Foundation of a Theological Tradition* (Oxford: Oxford University Press, 2000), 39–78.

of the Reformation era and those of the post-Reformation era. For as much as critics claim that scholasticism marred post-Reformation confessions, the evidence points in another direction. These brief examples illustrate the point that Reformed confessionalism was not a static phenomenon but rather one that responded and adapted to the needs of the church and to the polemical challenges of the day. In each of the cited examples, second-generation confessions did not add new doctrines to the first-generation confessional foundation but elaborated on already-existing doctrinal convictions by means of lengthier explanations and sharper terminology. This same pattern unfolds in the confessions of the post-Reformation era.

Early Orthodoxy (1565–ca. 1640)

Fewer confessions appeared in the Early Orthodox period than in the Reformation period, but these documents are nevertheless significant. In 1571, the Church of England adopted the Thirty-Nine Articles, which were based on the Forty-Two Articles that Thomas Cranmer (1489–1556) authored in 1553 under the reign of Edward VI (1537–53). The Forty-Two Articles were short-lived because Edward died immediately on the heels of their adoption and Queen Mary I (1516–58) nullified their use. When Mary died and Elizabeth I (1533–1603) ascended the throne, the new queen reinstituted the 1552 Book of Common Prayer and appealed to Matthew Parker (1504–75), the archbishop of Canterbury, to institute a confession of faith. Parker revised the Forty-Two Articles, reducing them to thirty-nine. In the process, he drew upon the Lutheran Confession of Württemberg (1552) of Johannes Brenz (1499–1570), which impacted articles 2, 5, 6, 10, 11, 12, and 20.[19] Cranmer and Parker were part of the broader Reformed tradition. Cranmer, for example, was friends with continental Reformed theologians such as Vermigli and Bucer. Nevertheless, this did not keep them and others in the Church of England from appealing to Lutheran theology.[20] The Thirty-Nine Articles, therefore,

---

19. Pelikan and Hotchkiss, *Creeds*, 2:526.
20. John Guy, *The Tudors: A Very Short Introduction* (Oxford: Oxford University Press, 2013), 64.

bear the marks of Reformed-Lutheran doctrinal cross-pollination and demonstrate that Reformed theologians looked beyond their own circle for insights.

One of the significant debates that arose in the wake of the adoption of the Thirty-Nine Articles took place at Cambridge University in 1595; it was over the doctrine of predestination. Two Cambridge students, Peter Baro (1534–99) and William Barrett (fl. 1595), objected to the common Reformed doctrine of predestination. Barrett preached a controversial sermon at the university church that triggered a response by university authorities. This response came in the form of nine articles on the doctrine of election drawn up by professor William Whitaker (1548–95).[21] Known as the Lambeth Articles (1595), they were intended as an expansion on the Thirty-Nine Articles (which already affirmed elements common to other Reformation-era confessions, including that predestination is the pretemporal decree of God unto everlasting life of certain individuals that brings the benefits of redemption in its wake). The Thirty-Nine Articles treat the doctrine pastorally by reminding readers that it is a teaching "full of sweet, pleasant, and unspeakable comfort to godly persons" (17). By way of contrast, the Lambeth Articles have a different tone and precision:

1. God from eternity has predestined some men to life, and reprobated some to death.

2. The moving or efficient cause of predestination to life is not the foreseeing of faith, or of perseverance, or of good works, or of anything innate in the person of the predestined, but only the will of the good pleasure of God.

3. There is a determined and certain number of predestined, which cannot be increased or diminished.

4. Those not predestined to salvation are inevitably condemned on account of their sins.

5. A true, lively, and justifying faith, and the sanctifying Spirit of God, is not lost nor does it pass away either totally or finally in the elect.

---

21. W. B. Patterson, *William Perkins and the Making of a Protestant England* (Oxford: Oxford University Press, 2014), 78–79.

6. The truly faithful man—that is, one endowed with justifying faith—is sure by full assurance of faith of the remission of sins and his eternal salvation through Christ.

7. Saving grace is not granted, is not made common, is not ceded to all men, by which they might be saved, if they wish.

8. No one can come to Christ unless it be granted to him, and unless the Father draws him: and all men are not drawn by the Father to come to the Son.

9. It is not in the will or the power of each and every man to be saved.

These lack the pastoral warmth of the Thirty-Nine Articles, but the university context and academic nature of the dispute explain their terse tenor. And while these articles arguably expand upon article 17, there are some minor differences. Article 17 speaks only of predestination to eternal life, whereas the Lambeth Articles explicitly present a double predestination: election and reprobation.[22] The Lambeth Articles were approved by the university but never endorsed by Queen Elizabeth. Some considered them an appendix to the Thirty-Nine Articles, but the lack of regal adoption mitigated their influence in the Church of England. They did, however, influence the Irish Articles (1615).

When the Church of Ireland wanted their own confession of faith, they imposed upon the head of the theological faculty at Trinity College, James Ussher (1581–1656), who would later become archbishop of Armagh. Ussher drew upon both the Thirty-Nine Articles and the Lambeth Articles as source documents.[23] This practice, which we have seen before, shows that authors of confessions were not keen on creating confessions de novo but instead employed the insights and work of those who went before them. The Irish Articles address their points of doctrine as thoroughly as do the Thirty-Nine Articles, and in 104 articles, they cover doctrines from God to the eschaton

22. Patterson, *Protestant England*, 79.
23. Pelikan and Hotchkiss, *Creeds*, 2:551; see also Alan Ford, *James Ussher: Theology, History, and Politics in Early-Modern Ireland and England* (Oxford: Oxford University Press, 2007), 85–103.

(following a pattern established by Reformation-era confessions such as the French, Belgic, and Second Helvetic). Like earlier confessions, the Irish Articles include a list of canonical books and exclude the Apocrypha (1–3). Subsequent articles address the need for the translation (4), perspicuity (5), and sufficiency of Scripture (6) and affirm a biblically subordinated church tradition by endorsing the Nicene, Athanasian, and Apostles' Creeds (7). These are natural additions in the wake of the Tridentine statements on Scripture.

But some might accuse Ussher of importing speculative scholastic sophistry into the Irish Articles with his treatment of predestination. Unlike the Thirty-Nine Articles, which cover predestination in a single article (17), Ussher presents seven articles on the doctrine. But far from needless academic abstractions, these seven articles reflect the development of the doctrine in both the Thirty-Nine Articles and the Lambeth Articles. Ussher was content to incorporate insights from both confessions, but the recent Cambridge controversy over predestination undoubtedly occupied his mind. That is, doctrinal controversies feature claims and counterclaims, and in each cycle of debate, doctrinal formulations acquire greater precision in order to refute heterodoxy. Hence, Ussher's articles on predestination address these controversy-necessitated subtopics: double predestination (12), the pretemporal origins of election (13), God as the moving cause (14), the supremacy of God's will (15), and the pastoral comfort of the doctrine of predestination (16–17). But even then, Ussher mitigates some of the scholastic turns of phrase by identifying God as the "cause moving" (14) rather than as the "moving or efficient cause" (Lambeth Articles, 2). Therefore, greater elaboration and precision is not infidelity to the theology of the Reformation but the side effect of doctrinal controversy.

This same pattern marks the infamous Canons of Dort (1619). Over the years, few confessional documents have been more vilified than the canons—accused of being speculative, predestinarian, scholastic, and unfaithful to the theology of Calvin.[24] Yet, among these critics, few acknowledge two important facts. First, the five

24. See, e.g., Brian G. Armstrong, *Calvinism and the Amyraut Heresy: Protestant Scholasticism and Humanism in Seventeenth-Century France* (1969; repr., Eugene, OR: Wipf & Stock, 2004).

articles of the canons were a direct response to the five Remonstrant articles. In other words, the international convocation of Reformed theologians did not gather of their own accord to write a confession on the doctrine of predestination; rather, they congregated to respond specifically to an ecclesiastical gravamen. Second, Remonstrants such as Jacob Arminius (1560–1609) and Simon Episcopius (1583–1643) were reportedly interested in revising the Belgic Confession to accommodate their views.[25] Some have disputed this, but if untrue, the fact still remains that Arminius and Episcopius wanted the church to read the Belgic Confession in a manner that would accommodate their views.[26] The synod, therefore, addressed the Remonstrant articles point by point with affirmations and rejections to ensure there was no question regarding the right interpretation of the Belgic Confession's article on predestination. All of this is to say that the Canons of Dort represent a defense of the Reformation doctrine of predestination, not an addition to, expansion of, or deviation from it. Even on the dreaded "limited atonement," the synod did not introduce anything new but employed a common medieval sufficiency-efficiency distinction regarding the extent of Christ's satisfaction that dates back to Peter Lombard (1096–1160) and was employed by Calvin.[27] Where Dort differed from the Remonstrants was in coordinating election and the atonement to determine the extent of the application of Christ's work.[28]

25. Theodoor Marius van Leeuwen, "Introduction: Arminius, Arminianism, and Europe," in *Arminius, Arminianism, and Europe: Jacobus Arminius (1559/60–1609)*, ed. Theodoor Marius van Leeuwen, Keith D. Stanglin, and Marijke Tolsma (Leiden: Brill, 2009), xvii; Nicholas Fornerod, "'The Canons of the Synod Had Shot Off the Advocate's Head': A Reappraisal of the Genevan Delegation at the Synod of Dort," in *Revisiting the Synod of Dordt (1618–1619)*, ed. Aza Goudriaan and Fred van Lieburg (Leiden: Brill, 2011), 188–89.

26. Keith D. Stanglin, *Arminius on the Assurance of Salvation: The Context, Roots, and Shape of the Leiden Debate, 1603–1609* (Leiden: Brill, 2007), 242.

27. Peter Lombard, *The Sentences Book 3: On the Incarnation of the Word*, trans. Giulio Silano (Toronto: PIMS, 2008), 20.5; John Calvin, *The Gospel according to St. John 11–21 and the First Epistle of John*, ed. David W. Torrance and T. F. Torrance (Grand Rapids: Eerdmans, 1994), 244; see also Richard A. Muller, *Christ and the Decree: Christology and Predestination in Reformed Theology from Calvin to Perkins* (Grand Rapids: Baker Academic, 2008), 34.

28. Richard A. Muller, *Calvin and the Reformed Tradition: On the Work of Christ and the Order of Salvation* (Grand Rapids: Baker Academic, 2012), 60–61; see also

But even then, there were a number of differences in how delegates accounted for the extent of Christ's satisfaction.[29]

Some might counter that the Irish Articles make a decisive break from the Reformation because this is the first confession to codify the covenants of works and grace. The covenant of works teaches that God and Adam were in covenant in the pre-fall context, and once Adam and Eve fell, God made a second covenant with them, the covenant of grace. The covenant of works was not formally introduced into Reformed theology until the last decade of the sixteenth century.[30] Next to the doctrine of the definite extent of Christ's satisfaction, the covenant of works is one of the more pilloried of those doctrines that are often viewed as intrusions of scholasticism into the Reformed confessional tradition.[31] The accusation that the covenant of works is a scholastic imposition usually rests on the assumption that Early Orthodox theologians first built their systems and then rummaged through the Scriptures to justify their claims.[32] Others have argued that the prevalence of covenant-making as a political and social practice led theologians to read the concept into the Scriptures and thereby create the covenants of works and grace.[33] Still others believe that the covenant of works rests on thin exegetical ice because only one text potentially speaks of an Adamic covenant (Hosea 6:7).[34] This is a complex issue that this brief section cannot sufficiently

W. Robert Godfrey, "Tensions Within International Calvinism: The Debate on the Atonement at the Synod of Dort, 1618–19" (PhD diss., Stanford University, 1974).

29. Muller, *Calvin and the Reformed Tradition*, 126–60.

30. See J. V. Fesko, *The Covenant of Works: Origins, Development, and Reception* (Oxford: Oxford University Press, 2020).

31. Holmes Rolston III, *John Calvin versus the Westminster Confession* (Richmond: John Knox, 1972), 23.

32. See, e.g., the negative comments in Philip Schaff, introduction to *Institutes of the Christian Religion*, by Emmanuel V. Gerhart, 2 vols. (New York: A. C. Armstrong & Son, 1891), 1:13; and contrast them with the analysis in Richard A. Muller and Rowland S. Ward, *Scripture and Worship: Biblical Interpretation and the Directory for Public Worship* (Phillipsburg, NJ: P&R, 2007), 3–84.

33. See, e.g., James B. Torrance, "Covenant or Contract? A Study of the Theological Background of Worship in Seventeenth-Century Scotland," *Scottish Journal of Theology* 23, no. 1 (1970): 51–76.

34. See, e.g., John Murray, "The Adamic Administration," in *Collected Writings of John Murray*, vol. 2, *Systematic Theology* (Edinburgh: Banner of Truth, 1977), 47–59, esp. 49–50.

cover, but it will suffice to show that the inclusion of the covenant of works demonstrates two important points of continuity between the Reformation-era confessions and Early Orthodoxy. First, with the Reformation-era confessions, those advocating for the inclusion of the covenant of works affirmed the chief authority of the Scriptures over tradition. Those opposing its inclusion implicitly claimed that the Reformation-era confessions created an unchanging norm and that the slightest deviation would represent a betrayal of its theology. But if Early Orthodox theologians reflected on and exegeted the Scriptures and came to the conviction that the covenant of works was a biblical doctrine, should they not have included it in their confessions? If Ussher was truly committed to the doctrine of Scripture advocated by Reformation-era confessions, then it was incumbent upon him to include the covenant of works in the Irish Articles. To oppose scripturally informed modifications of doctrine beyond the Reformation would be to elevate tradition over Scripture, thereby betraying the principles of the Reformation.

Second, many of the building blocks for the doctrine of the covenant of works appear in Reformation-era theological works. Even though Calvin is not the normative theologian for the Reformed tradition in the same way that Luther is for Lutheranism, he teaches a concept of natural law and identifies covenantal elements in the pre-fall Adamic context.[35] The fact that Calvin identifies the trees of the garden as sacraments, a chief indicator of the presence of a covenant, is an element of continuity between Reformation and Early Orthodox theology.[36] Considering the many substantive similarities between Reformation and Early Orthodox confessions, it is clear that Ussher's inclusion of the covenant of works in the Irish Articles represents a legitimate development in harmony with Reformation-era confessions.

35. John Calvin, *Institutes of the Christian Religion*, trans. Henry Beveridge (Grand Rapids: Eerdmans, 1957), 2.2.22; 2.7.1.
36. John Calvin, *1 Corinthians*, CNTC, ed. T. F. Torrance and David W. Torrance (1960; repr., Grand Rapids: Eerdmans, 1996), 249; see also Peter A. Lillback, *The Binding of God: Calvin's Role in the Development of Covenant Theology* (Grand Rapids: Baker Academic, 2001), 276–304.

High Orthodoxy (ca. 1640–1700)

In the period of High Orthodoxy, the Westminster Confession of Faith stands out as the most influential confessional document because it was created to unify England, Scotland, and Ireland and was also adopted by congregational and Baptist churches in modified form in the Savoy Declaration (1658) and Second London Confession (1689). Moreover, denominations still adhere to this confession in the present day. Its popularity has made the confession the object of both praise and criticism. Critics have identified it as a scholastic bastardization of the pristine theology of the Reformation. T. F. Torrance has called it the "great confession of Calvinist scholasticism which brought into quasi-creedal form the core of the systematized doctrine of the great Reformed dogmaticians of the early post-Calvin era."[37] Torrance's statement reveals two assumptions that underlie his criticisms of the confession: First, that Calvin serves as the normative theologian for the Reformed tradition (evident in Torrance's use of the term *Calvinist* and his claim that the confession codifies the theology of the "early post-Calvin era"). With this assumption, critics accuse the Westminster Confession of embodying not Calvin's theology but that of his successors. The second assumption is that scholasticism is both a method and a certain precision in the presentation of doctrinal positions. With this assumption, critics accuse the confession of embodying scholasticism. But both of these assumptions are incorrect.

As common as the term *Calvinism* is, the idea that Calvin is the fount of the Reformed tradition is mostly the result of mythology and artificial historical narratives generated by historians and theologians who do not like the Westminster Confession.[38] Torrance lists the influences on the assembly as Theodore Beza (1519–1605), Girolamo Zanchi (1516–90), Johannes Piscator (1546–1625), Gulielmus Bucanus (d. 1603), Bartholomäus Keckermann (ca. 1571–1608), Amandus Polanus (1561–1610), Johannes Wollebius (1589–1629), Zacharias

---

37. T. F. Torrance, *Scottish Theology: From John Knox to John McLeod Campbell* (London: T&T Clark, 1996), 125.

38. Richard A. Muller, "Demoting Calvin: The Issue of Calvin and the Reformed Tradition," in *John Calvin, Myth and Reality: Images and Impact of Geneva's Reformer*, ed. Amy Nelson Burnett (Eugene, OR: Cascade Books, 2011), 3–17.

Ursinus (1534–83), William Ames (1576–1633), and Antonius Walaeus (1573–1639). Calvin's absence from Torrance's list is telling. For the better part of a generation, scholars like Torrance have pitted Calvin against the Calvinists. Torrance, for example, notes, "The *Confession of Faith* does not manifest the spiritual freshness and freedom, or the evangelical joy, of the *Scots Confession* of 1560."[39] Such a criticism says more about Torrance's personal preferences than it does about the two confessions. Torrance does not factor in the circumstances surrounding the creation of the confessions. In 1560, the Scottish Parliament commissioned John Knox (ca. 1514–72) and five other pastors to write a Reformed confession. According to Knox, they wrote the document, and the parliament adopted it in only four days and with hardly any objection.[40] These circumstances are dramatically different from those surrounding the Westminster Confession, which was written over a period of three years (1644–46) by more than one hundred participants. To a large degree, the confession's specificity is the result of the rather mundane and practical necessity of having to please the scores of participants in the assembly (whereas only six men had to agree on the wording of the Scots Confession). Another important fact that escapes Torrance is that Knox and his coauthors drew upon many different sources to compose their confession. Indeed, Calvin and his *Institutes* were among the many sources consulted, as were the French, First Helvetic, and Augsburg Confessions, the Confession of Faith Used in the English Congregations in Geneva (1556), the First Confession of Basel (1531), the Geneva Catechism (1541/42), and the Forty-Two Articles (1553).[41] Calvin was a prominent source. But he was ultimately one source among many, including some of the authors of the above-cited confessions: Bullinger, Melanchthon, Cranmer, Beza, Viret, and Oswald Myconius (1488–1552). Unlike the Lutheran tradition, the Reformed tradition has never accorded any one theologian normative status.

39. Torrance, *Scottish Theology*, 127.
40. Pelikan and Hotchkiss, *Creeds*, 2:387; Jane Dawson, *John Knox* (New Haven: Yale University Press, 2015), 200–204.
41. Pelikan and Hotchkiss, *Creeds*, 2:387.

Furthermore, despite Torrance's claims, the Westminster Confession does not embody scholasticism. Torrance operates with the assumption that scholasticism is both a method and a certain precision in the presentation of doctrinal positions. Unlike the Scots Confession, the Westminster was supposedly "a rational explanation of Protestant theology composed in fulfillment of a constitutional establishment, reflecting the ridged dogmatism of the Synod of Dort."[42] However, despite the popularity of the claim, the Westminster Confession is not scholastic. It was written during the era of the use of the scholastic method, but it does not itself follow the method. The Westminster divines themselves said that they did not want to include scholastic, or academic, debates in a confession of faith.[43] All one has to do is compare the Westminster Confession with the *Institutes* of Francis Turretin (1623–87) to see the difference in genre. In true scholastic fashion, Turretin poses a question; states his view; presents the state of the question; and offers relevant exegesis, definition of terms, theological exposition, and refutation of erroneous views.[44] The confession, on the other hand, is a positive declaration of doctrine and parallels its accompanying catechisms, which present the same information in question and answer format for the sake of doctrinal instruction for people in the church.[45]

To be sure, even though the confession is not strictly scholastic, it does bear the discrete marks of the scholastic method in its carefully presented statements—the natural products of academically trained theologians. But the confession's concern for clarity, precision of definition, and logical order echo earlier, Reformation-era confessions such as the French, Belgic, and Second Helvetic. Moreover, two other factors required greater doctrinal precision: (1) distinguishing heterodoxy from orthodoxy in ongoing theological debates and (2) satisfying the consciences of the more than one hundred participants.

42. Torrance, *Scottish Theology*, 127.
43. Chad Van Dixhoorn, ed., *Minutes and Papers of the Westminster Assembly, 1643–1653*, 5 vols. (Oxford: Oxford University Press, 2012), sess. 520, 3:690.
44. See Francis Turretin, *Institutes of Elenctic Theology*, 3 vols. (Phillipsburg, NJ: P&R, 1992–97), 2.5.1–36.
45. Richard A. Muller, *After Calvin: Studies in the Development of a Theological Tradition* (Oxford: Oxford University Press, 2003), 27.

The Cambridge controversy over predestination that led to the creation of the Lambeth Articles influenced the Irish Articles, which in turn made their mark on the Westminster Confession. Note the similarities between the two opening statements in the respective confessions:

Irish Articles (1615)	Westminster Confession of Faith (1646)
God from all eternity did, by his unchangeable counsel, ordain whatsoever in time should come to pass; yet so, as thereby no violence is offered to the wills of the reasonable creatures, and neither the liberty nor the contingency of the second causes is taken away, but established rather (11).	God from all eternity did, by the most wise and holy Counsell of his own Will, freely, and unchangeably ordaine whatsoever comes to passe: yet so as thereby neither is God the Author of sin, nor is violence offered to the will of the Creatures, nor is the Liberty or contingencie of second Causes taken away, but rather established (3.1).[46]

The parallels between the two paragraphs reveal that the Westminster divines lifted this statement from the Irish Articles because they believed it was still relevant given the ongoing influence of Remonstrant views on predestination.[47] Traces of the scholastic method do appear in these two statements, with the invocation of secondary causality and contingency. But these concepts and terminology also appear in Calvin's *Institutes*, where he explains the relationship between the decree and human freedom.[48] One might accuse the divines of being overly academic in a document intended for people in the pew. But at the same time, they preserve important points of doctrine on theological topics of pastoral concern, such as divine sovereignty and human responsibility.

The same attention to detail marks other portions of the confession, including where it treats the topics of sanctification and the law. The divines provide a very specific exposition of sanctification and

---

46. *The Humble Advice of the Assembly of Divines, Now by Authority of Parliament Sitting at Westminster, Concerning a Confession of Faith* (London, 1647).
47. See Nicholas Tyacke, *Anti-Calvinists: The Rise of English Arminianism, ca. 1590–1640* (Oxford: Clarendon, 1987).
48. Calvin, *Institutes*, 1.16.9.

the law because antinomianism was a significant doctrinal problem during the assembly's deliberations. Their doctrinal precision was driven not by rigid dogmatism but by pastoral concern.[49] Among the communications received by the assembly, one letter complained about the sermons and books that were spreading antinomianism "in and about the citty of London" and perverting the "doctrines of free grace, justification by faith in Christ & of sanctification." The petitioners were concerned that antinomians would "soone draw millions of soules to cast off the whole morall law of God."[50] But antinomianism was not a new threat; noted Scottish divine Samuel Rutherford (ca. 1600–1661) traced refutations of antinomianism from Paul to Calvin's debates with the Libertines, Luther's challenge to Johannes Agricola (1494–1566), and Reformed responses to Anabaptist theologians such as Thomas Müntzer (ca. 1489–1525) and Hans Denck (ca. 1495–1527).[51] The divines did not, therefore, expand the scope of doctrine beyond Reformation parameters in their efforts to combat antinomianism; they echoed the Reformation-era teaching in their own historical context.

One of the last confessions of High Orthodoxy was the Formula Consensus Helvetica (1675), coauthored by Francis Turretin and Johannes Heidegger (1633–98). They wrote this confession to counteract perceived corrosive effects of doctrine emanating from the Academy of Saumur, such as the hypothetical universalism of Moïse Amyraut (1596–1664), the doctrine of mediate imputation put forward by Josué de la Place (ca. 1596–1665 or 1655), the rejection of the authority of the Masoretic vowel points advocated by Louis Cappel (1585–1658), and the threefold doctrine of the covenants advanced by Moïse Amyraut and John Cameron (ca. 1579–1625).[52] Advocates of these Sal-

49. Whitney Greer Gamble, "'If Christ Fulfilled the Law, We Are Not Bound': The Westminster Assembly against English Antinomian Soteriology, 1643–47" (PhD diss., University of Edinburgh, 2014).

50. John Lightfoot, "A Briefe Journal of Passages in the Assembly of Divines," August 20, 1643, in Chad Van Dixhoorn, "Reforming the Reformation: Theological Debate at the Westminster Assembly, 1643–52," 7 vols. (PhD diss., Cambridge University, 2004), 2:26.

51. Samuel Rutherford, *A Survey of the Spiritual Antichrist* 1.3 (London, 1648), 6.

52. Philip Schaff, *The Creeds of Christendom*, 3 vols. (Grand Rapids: Baker, 1990), 1:477–89.

murian views had been stirring up controversy in Geneva since the mid-seventeenth century, and church officials believed a confessional statement addressing the issues was necessary. Once Heidegger and Turretin composed the Formula Consensus Helvetica, Basel, Zurich, Bern, Neuchâtel, and Geneva adopted it by 1679. But opinions were sufficiently diversified that support for it was less than unanimous.

Despite its rapid adoption, some ministers refused to sign the confession and were allowed by the Swiss churches to dissent so long as they did not publicly contradict the confession.[53] Dissenters believed that the confession unduly narrowed the boundaries of orthodoxy even though proponents argued that it merely explained elements of the Second Helvetic Confession. On issues such as imputation, the Formula Consensus arguably elaborates on matters presented in the Second Helvetic Confession, but other issues cannot escape the dissenters' criticism. No creed before or after the Formula Consensus codified views related to the vowel points of the Masoretic text.[54] Reformers such as Luther and Calvin did not extend divine inspiration to the vowel points but viewed them as a reading aid to the un-pointed Hebrew text. Later High Orthodox theologians such as Turretin believed the vowel points were inspired. Pressure generated by polemics with Roman Catholic theologians raised the difference of opinion to doctrinal status. Jesuit theologian Robert Bellarmine (1542–1621) challenged the doctrine of *sola Scriptura* partially on the basis of the unintelligibility of the Hebrew text.[55] When Cappel seemingly sided with Roman Catholic critics, Reformed theologians were pressed to respond.

On the whole, High Orthodox hermeneutics stood in continuity with Reformation-era methods, though they were more specific on the status of the vowel points. High Orthodox theologians believed that inspiration and authority extended to the text itself—down to individual words and letters, even to tiny jots and tittles, even to vowel

---

53. James I. Good, *History of the Swiss Reformed Church Since the Reformation* (Philadelphia: Publication and Sunday School Board of the Reformed Church in the United States, 1913), 166–67.

54. For what follows, see Muller, *After Calvin*, 146–55.

55. Robert Bellarmine, *Controversies of the Christian Faith* 2.2, trans. Kenneth Baker (Saddle River, NJ: Keep the Faith, 2016), 105–10.

points. Unlike their Reformation-era counterparts, High Orthodox theologians wrestled with a growing body of Hebrew manuscripts and variant textual readings, and they sought to defend *sola Scriptura* in the face of these developments. Some High Orthodox theologians were unable to separate new methods of textual criticism from the views associated with Roman Catholic opponents. But others were able to adapt to the textual sea change. Theologians such as Richard Baxter (1615–91) adhered to *sola Scriptura* and argued for the authority and inspiration of the *autographa* (original copies)—the correct readings of which, he believed, could be established through textual criticism among the various extant manuscripts.[56] The Swiss churches erred, however, not so much in advocating for the inspiration of the vowel points but in making this highly debatable issue a matter of confessional orthodoxy.

At a time when Europe was still reeling over the confessionally drawn battle lines and the devastation left by the Thirty Years' War (1618–48), when the execution of Charles I (1600–1649) was still fresh in the minds of many, theologians and philosophers were calling for more theological toleration, not less. Its mediocre reception was immediate evidence that the Formula Consensus was a confessional overreach. Only seven years after its publication, candidates for the ministry in Lausanne merely had to subscribe to the formula *quatenus* (in so far as) it agreed with the Bible. From 1675 to 1700, one-third of all ministerial candidates were allowed to opt out of subscribing to the formula. In 1686, the elector Frederick William of Brandenburg (1620–88) pressured the Swiss churches to rescind the formula because he wanted the Salmurian refugees streaming into the country after the revocation of the Edict of Nantes (which had established legal toleration for Protestants in France) to feel welcome in the Swiss churches despite their different views. By 1706, Turretin's son, Jean-Alphonse Turretin (1671–1737), had convinced the Company of Pastors at Geneva to abandon the formula. Only in Heidegger's Zurich did the confession persist until it was eventually scuttled in 1741.[57] In some respects, the Formula Consensus was

---

56. Richard Baxter, *The Practical Works of Richard Baxter*, 4 vols. (1846; repr., Morgan, PA: Soli Deo Gloria, 2000), 3:93.
57. Good, *Swiss Reformed Church*, 169–77, 188–89.

doomed because, in unprecedented fashion, it excessively narrowed the gates of orthodoxy. It was a confession too far.

Conclusion

On the whole, post-Reformation confessions stand in continuity with the confessions of the Reformation. The confessions of both eras exhibit the same doctrinal substance. But because of different circumstances, participants, controversies, and doctrinal developments, there are some accidental differences. The first of these confessions were forged in the heat of doctrinal controversy in the effort to legitimize the burgeoning Protestant Reformation. New creedal needs arose, however, as the Protestant churches began to educate their members and train new ministers. These needs led to more expansive statements; theologians were no longer writing occasional documents but collaborating on confessions that addressed the full scope of biblical doctrine. In addition to this, as the darkness of false teaching descended on the Reformed churches, theological light rose to meet it. Intra-Protestant and Reformed–Roman Catholic debates impacted confessions. Reformed confessions of the post-Reformation period included greater clarity and precision in their formulations in order to distinguish Reformed doctrine from Roman Catholic, Remonstrant, Lutheran, and Anabaptist teaching. Another factor is that, as the Reformed churches grew, responsibility for writing confessions was no longer in the hands of a small cadre of ministers but rested with churches, synods, and international gatherings of theologians. With more participants involved in the drafting of confessions, sharper statements, sometimes including intentionally ambiguous phrasing, were needed to win the support of the largest possible number of ministers. In the end, rigid dogmatism and scholasticism did not determine and taint post-Reformation confessions. Rather, much more mundane factors shaped them: education, dispute, and large-scale participation.

THREE

Causes of Deconfessionalization

Introduction

What are the reasons behind the large-scale atrophy of confessions of faith? This is a question that might lead us to examine the cultural climate in an effort to determine why present-day churches largely eschew confessions of faith.[1] But while such an investigation would undoubtedly yield an accurate account of why churches reject confessionalism, it would only identify the branches and leaves on the anticonfessional tree rather than pinpoint its trunk and roots. Therefore, this chapter digs into the historical soil of the sixteenth century to identify the initial objections to confessionalism and then traces the development of anticonfessionalism into the present day. In short, there are internal and external reasons why Protestant churches largely abandoned confessionalism. Theologically inspired violence, failure to exercise church discipline, and admitting mysticism into the church weakened confessionalism from within. And confessionalism

1. For excellent treatments of present-day anticonfessionalism, see Carl R. Trueman, *The Creedal Imperative* (Wheaton: Crossway, 2012), 21–49; R. Scott Clark, *Recovering the Reformed Confession: Our Theology, Piety, and Practice* (Phillipsburg, NJ: P&R, 2008), 39–118.

was debilitated from without by mysticism and by unbelief in the forms of autonomous rationalism and skepticism. As tempting as it might be to lay the blame for the demise of confessionalism on the nominal church and the influence of the unbelieving world, history shows that the confessional church bears part of the blame.

This chapter demonstrates the twofold origin of the large-scale demise of confessionalism. It first examines Reformation-era skepticism—an intellectual tool, employed polemically by both Roman Catholic and Protestant theologians, that eventually spiraled out of control when mixed with Enlightenment rationalism.[2] It then uncovers the connections between confessionalism and war, most notably the Thirty Years' War and the English Civil War. These wars were fought on confessional lines and did little more than shed much blood and sour opinions against confessions of faith. In the wake of the cataclysm of theologically inspired war, theologians and philosophers wanted to tear down confessional walls in the effort to promote religious toleration. The chapter then turns to the juggernaut of the Enlightenment, which played a tremendous role in the large-scale demise of confessionalism. The Kantian watershed of autonomous reason produced three events that further eroded confidence in confessions of faith—namely, the creation of the discipline of biblical theology, the advent of higher critical exegesis, and the rise of the modern German university. The corrosive effects of mysticism and pietism are also examined. And finally, a brief survey of present-day individualism is given. Contrary to popular belief, we have not transcended the philosophical categories of modernity; we do not live in a *postmodern* age. Rather, the philosophical categories of modernity still persist in heightened form. We live in a *hypermodern* age. Despite the collapse of confessionalism in our day, tracing the roots of its demise can help the small minority of remaining confessional churches both to avoid the errors of the past and to understand and engage meaningfully with unbelievers in the present.

2. The roots of skepticism lie not in the sixteenth century but in the ancient world, as the following exposition reveals. This chapter begins with the sixteenth century, but one could argue that all of the trends that appear in the 1500s have ancient roots and predecessors.

Skepticism

Given the fact that confessions of faith and the Reformation go hand in hand, people might be surprised to learn that there was opposition to creeds early in the sixteenth century. When Martin Luther (1483–1546) challenged the church's doctrine, not every critic of Rome agreed with his theological claims. A number of humanist scholars such as Thomas More (1478–1535) and Desiderius Erasmus of Rotterdam (1466/9–1536) criticized the Protestant movement because they feared that, fueled by its doctrine of *sola Scriptura*, it would breed fundamentalism—and that in this fundamentalist climate, humanist learning and freedom of inquiry would wither.[3] Luther and the other Reformers were not opposed to humanist scholarship, but they undoubtedly had different aims and goals for this knowledge.[4] Erasmian humanism had no doctrinal cast, whereas other forms of humanism came in different confessional frameworks, in either Lutheran, Roman Catholic, or Reformed varieties.[5] The differences between the two types of humanism (free agent versus confessional) emerged in the theological debate between Erasmus and Luther over the doctrine of free will.

In this debate, Luther referred to Erasmus as a skeptic because he was unwilling to decide certain theological issues.[6] Erasmus was not fond of theological certitude and thus willingly joined the ranks of the skeptics—though as a Catholic, he was willing to submit to the authority of Scripture and the decrees of the church. In short, Erasmus adopted the Pyrrhonist mode of argument, which required that one suspend judgment in the face of a challenging issue.[7] Pyrrhonist skepticism was documented by Sextus Empiricus (ca. 160–210) in his *Outlines of Pyrrhonism* and in the works of Cicero (106–43 BC).[8] As humanists scoured

---

3. Erika Rummel, *The Confessionalization of Humanism in Reformation Germany* (Oxford: Oxford University Press, 2000), 30.
4. Rummel, *Confessionalization of Humanism*, 39–43.
5. Rummel, *Confessionalization of Humanism*, 49.
6. Rummel, *Confessionalization of Humanism*, 54.
7. Rummel, *Confessionalization of Humanism*, 56.
8. Rummel, *Confessionalization of Humanism*, 56; Anton M. Matytsin, *The Specter of Skepticism in the Age of Enlightenment* (Baltimore: Johns Hopkins University Press, 2016), 26; Sextus Empiricus, *Outlines of Pyrrhonism*, LCL, trans. R. G. Bury (Cambridge, MA: Harvard University Press, 1966).

ancient literature, they discovered Pyrrhonist skepticism and used it as an engine of theological warfare. Erasmus despised doctrinal disputes because he believed consensus was the essential criterion in doctrinal truth.[9] Luther, on the other hand, railed against Erasmus for his skepticism: "Let Skeptics and Academics keep well away from us Christians, but let there be among us 'assertors' twice as unyielding as the Stoics themselves." To support his claims of certainty, Luther appealed to texts such as Romans 10:10 ("For with the heart one believes and is justified, and with the mouth one confesses and is saved") and Matthew 10:32 ("Everyone who acknowledges me before men, I also will acknowledge before my Father").[10] Luther insisted, "What is more miserable than uncertainty? . . . Take away assertions and you take away Christianity."[11] Luther derided Erasmus for claiming loyalty to the Scriptures while hiding behind a cloud of skepticism.[12] "So far am I from delighting in the opinion of the Skeptics," Luther wrote, "that, whenever the infirmity of the flesh will permit, I will not only consistently adhere to and assert the sacred writings, everything and in all parts of them, but I will also wish to be as certain as possible in things that are not vital and that lie outside of Scripture."[13] Erasmus wanted the freedom to believe or not believe certain doctrines and did not want the constraints of a confessional framework, whereas Luther was of the polar opposite opinion. Skepticism motivated Erasmus, and a creedal impulse drove Luther; Erasmus never played a role in the creation of a confession or catechism, whereas Luther was involved in both—with the Augsburg Confession (1530) and his Small Catechism (1529) and Large Catechism (1529).[14]

Erasmus and Luther represent the establishment of two different Reformation-era trajectories: skepticism and confessionalism. The

9. Rummel, *Confessionalization of Humanism*, 57.

10. Martin Luther, *On the Bondage of the Will*, in *Luther and Erasmus: Free Will and Salvation*, Library of Christian Classics, ed. and trans. E. Gordon Rupp (Louisville: Westminster John Knox, 1969), 106. For what follows, see Rummel, *Confessionalization of Humanism*, 57.

11. Luther, *Bondage of the Will*, 106, 108.

12. Luther, *Bondage of the Will*, 107.

13. Luther, *Bondage of the Will*, 108.

14. See Robert Kolb and Timothy Wengert, eds., *The Book of Concord: The Confessions of the Evangelical Lutheran Church* (Minneapolis: Fortress, 2000), 27–106, 345–480.

die was cast, and skepticism became a competing paradigm against the spirit of confessionalism. Sebastian Castellio (1515–63) tried to employ skepticism as a weapon against John Calvin's doctrine of election. Castellio rejected the doctrine of the perspicuity of Scripture and was therefore reluctant to agree with Calvin's doctrine of predestination. His belief in the obscurity of the Scriptures extended to his pleas for theological toleration. He objected to Geneva's insistence on doctrinal conformity: "If anyone disagrees with their interpretations, institutions, and ceremonies, they put him in chains on the very same day, at the earliest possible time. Then, in chains, he argues and defends himself, and if he does not agree with them and does not go against his own convictions, that is, if he is not prepared to lie, he must die . . . or certainly go into exile."[15] Castellio was a committed theological skeptic and even wrote a book on the topic, *On the Art of Doubting and Trusting, Not Knowing and Knowing* (1544).[16] Calvin's lieutenant, Theodore Beza (1519–1605), responded to Castellio and rejected his skepticism as unbiblical and un-Christian.[17]

Confessionalism flourished in the latter half of the sixteenth century with the creation of numerous major confessions and catechisms, including the French Confession (1559), Belgic Confession (1561), Heidelberg Catechism (1563), and Second Helvetic Confession (1566). But skepticism nevertheless received an infusion of life with the republication of Sextus Empiricus's *Outlines of Pyrrhonism* in 1562. Both Protestants and Roman Catholics used Pyrrhonism as a weapon against one another. Roman Catholics cast the shadow of skepticism over human reason, which they said required the church's indispensable assistance as authoritative interpreter of the Word of God. Francisco Suárez (1548–1617) rejected the Protestant doctrine of the perspicuity of Scripture and relied on Sextus Empiricus's views to do so. Protestants, conversely, used skepticism against Roman Catholic interpretations of Scripture, claiming that such interpretations shouldn't be trusted because they were made by fallible human authorities.[18] But even though both Protestants and Roman Catholics

15. As quoted in Rummel, *Confessionalization of Humanism*, 67.
16. Rummel, *Confessionalization of Humanism*, 68.
17. Rummel, *Confessionalization of Humanism*, 71.
18. Matytsin, *Specter of Skepticism*, 26–28.

were adherents to confessional theology, they were unable to contain the Pyrrhonism.

Skeptics began to use Pyrrhonian doubt to challenge the veracity and inspiration of the Scriptures. The most notorious employment of Pyrrhonian skepticism was the *Tractatus Theologico-Politicus* (1670) by Baruch Spinoza (1632–77).[19] Both Protestant and Roman Catholic theologians vigorously opposed Pyrrhonian skepticism, but the genie was out of the bottle and spread among many philosophers and theologians.[20] The best-known disseminator of Pyrrhonism was Reformed Huguenot theologian Pierre Bayle (1647–1706). Critics of skepticism identified Bayle's *Historical and Critical Dictionary* as one of the chief sources of the Pyrrhonian infection.[21] Bayle's critics described his dictionary as turning theology "into an art of speaking much and thinking little, of never understanding the views of others, of taking their thoughts as backward, and of not understanding oneself."[22] Other detractors claimed that Bayle's skepticism reduced morality to nothing more than a question of personal preference.[23] Despite these censures, Bayle's dictionary was the most widely purchased book in the latter half of the eighteenth century and was translated into German and English.[24] While some of Bayle's disparagers might have overstated their concerns, one effect of Bayle's Pyrrhonism was the spread of his theological irenicism. Bayle pleaded for religious toleration and promoted his own dissenting interpretations of the Bible against Roman Catholic and Reformed peers.[25] In other words, skepticism drove Bayle and others to eschew confessional restrictions.

On the one hand, religious toleration can generally be a good thing, given that no one should ever try to force conformity to a set of theological convictions. Disaster has resulted any time the church has taken up the sword to enforce religious conformity. On the other hand, religious toleration that eschews all theological boundaries can

---

19. Matytsin, *Specter of Skepticism*, 35.
20. Matytsin, *Specter of Skepticism*, 37.
21. Matytsin, *Specter of Skepticism*, 39; Pierre Bayle, *An Historical and Critical Dictionary*, 4 vols. (London: Hunt and Clarke, 1826).
22. Matytsin, *Specter of Skepticism*, 44.
23. Matytsin, *Specter of Skepticism*, 48.
24. Matytsin, *Specter of Skepticism*, 52.
25. Matytsin, *Specter of Skepticism*, 57.

be equally problematic. As the poet Robert Frost (1874–1963) once wrote in his famous poem "Mending Wall," "Fences make for good neighbors."[26] When religious toleration begins to tear down confessional walls, there is a danger of losing important biblical truths. Is Christ of a similar or the same essence as the Father? Is he *homoiousias* or *homoousias*? The early church erected a wall to distinguish orthodoxy from heresy, to affirm the biblical truth that the Son is fully God and fully human.[27] Such a confessional wall is necessary. But our walls should not be so high that no one can ever scale them. To be good neighbors, we should maintain our confessional fences but do so in a spirit of love and theological irenicism, always open to dialoguing and willing to remove fences if we find that they are unbiblical or unnecessary.

War

Bayle's pursuit of religious toleration was undoubtedly motivated by his Pyrrhonism. But another factor contributing to the demise of confessionalism was the specter of war. The Thirty Years' War (1618–48) and the English Civil War (1642–51) overlap with two of early modern Europe's great confessions: the Canons of Dort (1619) and the Westminster Standards (1648). The convergence of bloody warfare and confessionalism cannot be ignored and was unquestionably a factor in the large-scale demise of confessionalism later in Europe. In early modernity, confessionally drawn theological boundaries and violence went hand in hand.

During the reign of Queen Mary I (1553–58), nearly three hundred Protestant martyrs died for the faith. Conversely, Roman Catholics suffered under Protestant rule, adding yet more bricks to the wall dividing Protestants and Roman Catholics. On August 23, 1572, Roman Catholics slaughtered approximately three thousand French Huguenots. This event became known as the St. Bartholomew's Day

26. Robert Frost, "Mending Wall," in *Frost: Poems*, ed. John Hollander (New York: Knopf, 1997), 55–56.
27. See Donald Fairbairn and Ryan M. Reeves, *The Story of Creeds and Confessions: Tracing the Development of the Christian Faith* (Grand Rapids: Baker Academic, 2019), 48–79.

Massacre; it was a day that would live in infamy in Protestant hearts and minds. In 1588, Roman Catholic Spain sent its naval fleet to attack Protestant England, but superior English naval bombardment and a massive storm destroyed the majority of the Spanish fleet. On November 5, 1605, Guy Fawkes (1570–1606) was caught on the first floor of parliament trying to prepare several tons of explosives in his effort to blow the roof off parliament during its opening session when the king would be present. Fawkes wanted to decapitate the Protestant government and see a Roman Catholic monarch installed on England's throne.[28] This back-and-forth between confessional communities set the stage for two of the most significant wars in Europe's history—wars that left both Protestants and Catholics with blood on their hands.

The Thirty Years' War

The two sides of the Thirty Years' War were the confessionally defined Protestant Union (1608) and the Catholic League (1609). In the six terms of the Protestant Union, members agreed to defend one another if attacked and to not attack one another in books or sermons over doctrinal issues (though theologians were free to engage in disputations).[29] War was sparked when the Protestant citizens of Bohemia decided to show their disdain for their new Roman Catholic king, the archduke Ferdinand of Styria (1578–1637), by reenacting the Defenestration of Prague.[30] The original defenestration occurred in 1418 when Hussites cast church officials out of a large castle window and they plummeted to their deaths. On the bicentennial of this event, the Bohemian Protestants seized two leading Catholic nobles and reenacted the defenestration, though this time the victims landed in a pile of dung and emerged unharmed. Nevertheless, this roused the Catholic Bohemians, who raised an army of sixteen thousand men and invaded and captured the city of Pilsen, which eventually

---

28. Meic Pearse, *The Age of Reason: From the Wars of Religion to the French Revolution 1570–1789* (Grand Rapids: Baker Books, 2006), 43–47; Antonia Fraser, *Faith and Treason: The Story of the Gunpowder Plot* (New York: Anchor, 1997).

29. Pearse, *Age of Reason*, 152; Peter H. Wilson, *The Thirty Years War: A Sourcebook* (London: Palgrave Macmillan, 2010), 12–19.

30. Wilson, *Thirty Years War*, 35–36.

led to the re-Catholicization of Bohemia. More than one hundred thousand Protestants were exiled, and Jesuits took control of the once-Protestant University of Prague. These events snowballed into one of Europe's bloodiest conflicts in modern history. Participants would eventually sign the Treaty of Westphalia on October 24, 1648. But this peace could not erase the devastation of war. The war produced an estimated 8 million dead. One-third of the pre-war German population perished in the war. In Bohemia, only 6,000 of the original 35,000 villages were spared destruction and only 700,000 of the province's 2 million residents survived. In one German county, 75 percent of the population, 80 percent of the livestock, and 66 percent of the houses were destroyed. Population levels in the Holy Roman Empire would not return to pre-war levels until 1720. Germany and Europe would not experience devastation of this magnitude again until World War I (1914–18), nearly three hundred years later.[31]

The English Civil War

The geography of the English Civil War naturally limited the number of casualties; nevertheless, they were significant for what was—compared to mainland Europe—a relatively small island. There were nearly two hundred thousand military and civilian casualties during the eleven-year civil war.[32] But it was perhaps the regicide of Charles I (1600–1649) that had the greatest consequences. Among other issues, confessional commitments divided Charles from many of his subjects; the National Covenant (1638) expressed many of these concerns, including original sin, justification, sanctification, the law, sacraments, liturgy, degrees of consanguinity, and the like. The fear was that Charles was introducing Tridentine Roman Catholicism into Scotland.[33] The National Covenant was a declaration of theological war, drawn on confessional boundaries, that gave birth to a physical

---

31. Michael Clodfelter, *Warfare and Armed Conflicts: A Statistical Encyclopedia of Casualty and Other Figures, 1492–2015*, 4th ed. (Jefferson, NC: MacFarland & Company, 2017), 40; C. V. Wedgwood, *The Thirty Years War* (New York: New York Review Books, 2005); Richard Bonney, *The Thirty Years' War 1618–1648* (Oxford: Osprey, 2002).

32. Clodfelter, *Warfare and Armed Conflicts*, 52.

33. See the National Covenant in *The Westminster Confession of Faith* (1646; repr., Glasgow: Free Presbyterian Publications, 1995), 347–54.

war between Charles on the one side and Scotland and a majority of the English Parliament on the other. The lines distinguishing theological from political concerns were blurred, as is evident in the famous characterization by Robert Baillie (1602–62) of the alliance between the Scots and the English: "The English were for a civill League, we for a religious Covenant."[34] In other words, the Scots were interested in creating an alliance with the English in order to unite the British Isles under a single confession of faith, whereas the English were more interested in adding Scottish armies to their ranks to counter royalist forces. Regardless of the motivations, the Scots and the English united under the Solemn League and Covenant (1643), which, among other things, vowed to unite the British Isles in "doctrine, worship, discipline, and government" against their common enemies.[35] The desire for confessional unity propelled the proponents of the National Covenant to war and eventually regicide. Confession and warfare were inextricably intertwined—and, naturally, this has been disconcerting to critics of confessions.

The Effects of War

Thomas Hobbes (1588–1679) and John Locke (1632–1704) were two of the most vocal detractors of the confessional impulse and argued for religious toleration. Hobbes, in his famous *Leviathan* (1651), complained that covenant theology, natural law theory, and common law were the causes of the civil war between Charles and the Presbyterian parliament. He laid the blame at the feet of inflammatory Presbyterian preaching.[36] Hobbes believed their unnecessary doctrinal disputes flowed out of the universities and into the commonwealth.[37] Few controversies between the Presbyterians and royalist theologians such as Archbishop William Laud (1573–1645) were

---

34. Robert Baillie, "Letter to Mr. W. Spang, September 22, 1643," in *The Letters and Journals of Robert Baillie*, ed. David Laing, vol. 2 (Edinburgh, 1841), 90.
35. "Solemn League and Covenant," in *Westminster Confession of Faith*, 358–60.
36. Victoria Kahn, *Wayward Contracts: The Crisis of Political Obligation in England, 1640–1674* (Princeton: Princeton University Press, 2016), 135; Thomas Hobbes, *Leviathan*, ed. Richard Tuck (Cambridge: Cambridge University Press, 1996), 110–11.
37. Thomas Hobbes, *Behemoth*, ed. Paul Seaward (Oxford: Clarendon, 2010), 188.

over things necessary for salvation.[38] Hobbes challenges, "Is there any Controversy between Bishop and Presbyterian concerning the Divinity or Humanity of Christ, do either of them deny the Trinity, or any Article of the Creed? Does either party preach openly or write directly against Justice, Charity, Sobriety, or any other duty necessary to Salvation?"[39]

Hobbes recommended that Christianity focus on big-picture issues. In this he was following the example of Richard Allestree (ca. 1621–81), the Anglican Remonstrant theologian who wrote *The Whole Duty of Man, Laid Down in a Plain and Familiar Way for the Use of All* (1661), a work focused on practice and ethics rather than doctrine.[40] Hobbes believed that practice was more important than conflict-producing doctrine. Scholastic theology was too indebted to Aristotle and theological distinctions that "signifie nothing, but serve only to astonish the multitude of ignorant men."[41] The theologians of his day went far beyond the reforms of Martin Luther (1483–1545) and John Calvin (1509–64) and created a great number of sects as a result of their "many strange & many pernicious doctrins."[42] For Hobbes, confessional theology was a big-budget movie chock-full of special effects but lacking in both plot and acting. Hobbes found a sympathetic, like-minded ally in John Locke.

Locke famously argued for religious freedom in his *Letter Concerning Toleration* (1689).[43] Locke was raised as a Reformed Christian in the shadow of the English Civil War. When he was in school, he read James Ussher's writings on church polity and sat under the preaching of John Owen (1616–83). The execution of Charles I undoubtedly left an impression on the young Locke, who at the time was enrolled at the Westminster School, which was nestled in the confines of Westminster Abbey. When the king was executed at Westminster, the principal, Richard Busby (1606–95), called on the students to pray for the king's

38. Hobbes, *Behemoth*, 189.
39. Hobbes, *Behemoth*, 188.
40. Richard Allestree, *The Whole Duty of Man: Laid Down in a Plain and Familiar Way for the Use of All, but Especially for the Meanest Reader* (London, 1704).
41. Hobbes, *Behemoth*, 161.
42. Hobbes, *Behemoth*, 290–91.
43. John Locke, *A Letter Concerning Toleration*, in *The Works of John Locke*, 9 vols. (London, 1824), 5:1–58.

soul.[44] In other words, Locke was intimately familiar with the dark side of confessionalism. Another significant event in Locke's life was the Great Ejection, which followed the Act of Uniformity (1662). Upon the restoration of the monarchy, Charles II (1630–85) issued a decree that all ministers of the Church of England were required to subscribe to the Book of Common Prayer. Instead of bringing unity to the church, it only created more division. Over seventeen hundred ministers resigned or were ejected from their pulpits; approximately 5 to 20 percent of the English population followed these ministers and worshiped as nonconformists in independent churches.[45] Whether due to its association with the Presbyterian parliament during the civil war or due to the Act of Conformity, confessionalism made a lasting negative impression on Locke.

In his effort to combat the excesses of confessionalism, Locke wrote *A Letter on Toleration*, outlining the respective roles he believed the church and the magistrate should play concerning religion.[46] In it, Locke makes three claims regarding the necessity of religious toleration.[47] First, neither church nor magistrate should compel anyone by force to believe in doctrine.[48] This is because toleration for diverse theological views is supposed to lie at the very heart and mission of the church;[49] and in any case, the civil magistrate is ill-equipped to police theological convictions by physical force.[50] Second, the church is no longer the fulcrum for determining theological positions—the individual is. This means that no one is born into a church; one can only join by voluntary association. And once one joins, if "he finds anything wrong with its doctrine or unseemly in its ritual, he must have the same liberty to leave as he had to

44. John Marshall, *John Locke: Resistance, Religion and Responsibility* (Cambridge: Cambridge University Press, 1994), 1–6.

45. Marshall, *John Locke*, 33.

46. John Locke, *Locke on Toleration*, ed. Richard Vernon (Cambridge: Cambridge University Press, 2010), 3–46.

47. For an overview of Locke's views, see Marshall, *John Locke*, 33–72; Elissa B. Alzate, *Religious Liberty in a Lockean Society* (New York: Palgrave MacMillan, 2017), 29–62.

48. Locke, *Locke on Toleration*, 8.

49. Locke, *Locke on Toleration*, 9.

50. Locke, *Locke on Toleration*, 8.

enter."[51] Third, church doctrine should come only from the express statements of Scripture concerning salvation; mere mortals should not be allowed to impose their interpretations on the Scriptures and thereby draw doubtful doctrinal conclusions.[52] Locke illustrates this point with a hypothetical scenario involving an Arminian church and a Calvinist church in the city of Constantinople. He observes that each church would claim that it is the true church and the other is not: "For every church is orthodox in its own eyes, and in the eyes of others it is erroneous or heretical."[53] In such a situation, the magistrate should not get involved in the dispute but should ensure protection for both groups.

This illustration was not very hypothetical, as Locke likely gleaned it from reading the work of the Dutch jurist Hugo Grotius (1583–1645), including his *De Veritate Religionis Christianae* (1627). Grotius was imprisoned in the wake of the decrees of the Synod of Dort (1618–19).[54] He argued against detailed confessions of faith in *De Veritate*, which was silent even on the doctrine of the Trinity.[55] He believed that morality, rather than detailed confessions of faith, should be the Christian's chief concern.[56] According to Locke, "With regard to speculative doctrines and what are called articles of faith, which require only to be believed, there is no way that civil law can introduce them into a church."[57] Not even the much decried "conventicles"— small heterodox and heretical sects—should be subject to censure by the civil magistrate, according to Locke.[58] Such an opinion stands in stark opposition to the earlier views of Samuel Rutherford (ca. 1600–1661) and Thomas Edwards (1599–1647).[59] Their work uncovered the

51. Locke, *Locke on Toleration*, 9.
52. Locke, *Locke on Toleration*, 9.
53. Locke, *Locke on Toleration*, 14.
54. Jonathan I. Israel, *The Dutch Republic: Its Rise, Greatness, and Fall 1477–1806* (Oxford: Clarendon, 1995), 450–65.
55. Marshall, *John Locke*, 64; See Hugo Grotius, *The Truth of the Christian Religion*, ed. Maria Rosa Antognazza (Indianapolis: Liberty Fund, 2012).
56. Locke, *Locke on Toleration*, 11.
57. Locke, *Locke on Toleration*, 30.
58. Locke, *Locke on Toleration*, 37–38.
59. Samuel Rutherford, *A Survey of the Spiritual Antichrist* (London, 1648); Thomas Edwards, *The First and Second Part of Gangraena* (London, 1646); Edwards, *The Third Part of Gangraena* (London, 1646).

dangers and vices of these conventicles and claimed that they harmed the public peace and commonwealth (a claim Locke utterly rejected).[60]

Locke summarizes his view of religious toleration: "Is it permitted to worship God in the Roman manner? Let it be permitted in the Genevan form also."[61] For Locke, it is the height of arrogance to claim that any one church possesses the truth regarding salvation:

> I know that there are propositions which are so obviously consistent with Holy Scripture that no one can doubt that they follow from it, and there can be no quarrel about these. But you must not impose on others as a necessary article of faith anything that seems to you to follow by valid deduction from Holy Scripture, because you yourself believe it to be consistent with the rule of faith—unless you are willing to accept that other's people's view be imposed by equal right upon you, and you be compelled to accept and profess different and mutually conflicting doctrines from Lutherans, Calvinists, Remonstrants, Anabaptists, and other sects, doctrine which the manufacturers of creeds and systems and confessions are apt to impose upon their followers and preach as necessary and genuine inferences from Holy Scripture. I cannot help but wonder at the unholy arrogance of those who think that they can teach what is necessary to salvation more clearly and plainly than the Holy Spirit, who is the infinite and eternal wisdom.[62]

Locke distinguishes the clear statements about salvation in Scripture from the doctrines deduced from Scripture—deduced, that is, by what the Westminster Confession (1647) calls "good and necessary consequence" (1.6). He believes that matters of salvation are clear, but articles of faith, symbols, confessions, and systems are dubious and unwarranted.

Locke's influence on the development of political philosophy and theology has been significant. He swayed both confessional and anticonfessional theologians. Confessional theologians in the newly founded American Presbyterian church employed Locke's views on the separation of church and state in their revisions of the Westmin-

---

60. Locke, *Locke on Toleration*, 38.
61. Locke, *Locke on Toleration*, 40.
62. Locke, *Locke on Toleration*, 45.

ster Standards in 1788. With these revisions, the civil magistrate no longer had the authority to enforce religious doctrine:

> Yet, as nursing fathers, it is the duty of civil magistrates to protect the church of our common Lord, without giving the preference to any denomination of Christians above the rest, in such a manner that all ecclesiastical persons whatever shall enjoy the full, free, and unquestioned liberty of discharging every part of their sacred functions, without violence or danger. And, as Jesus Christ hath appointed a regular government and discipline in his church, no law of any commonwealth should interfere with, let, or hinder, the due exercise thereof, among the voluntary members of any denomination of Christians, according to their own profession and belief.

In Lockean fashion, the American Presbyterians also deleted "tolerating false religions" as a violation of the second commandment in question 109 of the Larger Catechism. In other words, the magistrate no longer had the responsibility to suppress heresy.[63] But even though Locke influenced Presbyterian confessionalism, his greater impact lies with his arguments in favor of deconfessionalization. The elevation of the individual over the church, the promotion of voluntary association, and the stripping away of so-called speculative doctrines (such as the Trinity) had a lasting effect on European and American cultures that would only grow in the Enlightenment.

The Enlightenment Juggernaut

The Thirty Years' War disfigured the European cultural, theological, and philosophical landscape. Theologians and philosophers wanted to free church and state from the confessional dogmas that they believed led to the war and hindered true progress. But the Enlightenment was

---

63. Guy Klett, ed., *Minutes of the Presbyterian Church in America: 1706–88*, Sept. 19, 1729, and May 26, 1788 (Philadelphia: Presbyterian Historical Society, 1976), 103–4, 635–37; Leah Farish, "The First Amendment's Religion Clauses: The Calvinist Document That Interprets Them Both," *Journal of Religion & Society* 12 (2010): 1–22; D. G. Hart, "American Presbyterianism: Exceptional," *Journal of Presbyterian History* 84, no. 1 (2006): 12–16.

not merely backlash against theologically inspired war; it was also motivated by the ascendency of rationalism.

Immanuel Kant (1724–1804) wrote his brief, famous essay "What Is Enlightenment?" (1784), which set the eighteenth-century course for the rejection of confessions. In the essay, Kant defines enlightenment as "the human being's emergence from his self-incurred minority [*Unmündigkeit*, or "immaturity"]." And he defines *immaturity* as a person's inability to make use of his or her own reason apart from direction from another.[64] When Kant illustrates immaturity, he appeals to different examples: "But I hear from all sides the cry: *Do not argue!* The officer says: Do not argue but drill! The tax official: Do not argue but pay! The clergyman: Do not argue but believe! . . . Everywhere there are restrictions on freedom." Thus people are subject to their own self-imposed immaturity.[65] Kant saw two evils in his day that required remedy: self-imposed restrictions and those imposed by others. He believed that the church fed both forms of limitation. The church told people what to believe, and people allowed the church to lead them around by the nose rather than outgrowing their immaturity and self-imposed limitations and thinking for themselves.

But Kant isn't satisfied with merely making some general criticisms against the church. He launches a broadside attack on confessionalism with several intellectual torpedoes. He recognizes that clergy are bound to preach and teach the established creeds of their churches; confessional conformity is the condition of their employment, after all. But he believes that clergy can also function as scholars, registering their own independent opinions with the wider world rather than only those of their confessionally constrained churches. In other words, Kant acknowledges that when ministers teach in their churches they are not free to teach as they truly believe; but when they promote their own opinions to the world, there should be nothing to bind their consciences. He believes they should be free to contradict the teachings of the churches they serve. In the public use of their reason,

---

64. Immanuel Kant, "An Answer to the Question: What Is Enlightenment?," in *Practical Philosophy*, Cambridge Edition of the Works of Immanuel Kant, trans. and ed. Mary J. Gregor (Cambridge: Cambridge University Press, 1999), 17.
65. Kant, "What Is Enlightenment?," 18.

therefore, ministers should enjoy unrestricted freedom to make use of reason and to speak as free agents.[66] Kant anticipates the question, What if ministers voluntarily bind themselves by oath to an unalterable creed in order to preserve a body of doctrine for their church? Kant specifically invokes the terms *synod* and *classis* ("as it calls itself among the Dutch"), which proves that he was generally familiar with the theology of the Reformation, ecclesiastical polities, and the practice of confession subscription. Nevertheless, even if voluntary, such a practice was unthinkable to him: "I say that this is quite impossible. Such a contract, concluded to keep all further enlightenment away from the human race forever, is absolutely null and void, even if it were ratified by the supreme power, by imperial diets and by the most solemn peace treaties."[67] For clergy to bind themselves to an unalterable confession would impede enlightenment and would be a crime against humanity, whose chief end is to progress in knowledge. According to Kant, succeeding generations of humanity are perfectly free to reject such ecclesiastical confessional commitments as unauthorized and sacrilegious.[68] Since confessions are a hindrance to enlightenment, clergy have the responsibility to deviate from their adopted creeds and to work their way out of intellectual barbarism.[69]

Kant is not the only one responsible for the rejection of confessions, but his brief essay captures the Enlightenment zeitgeist and its antipathy toward confessional theology. His essay also reveals the motivating factors behind the intellectual sea change. The eighteenth-century intelligentsia rejected the confessional ethos of the church as barbarism. Kantian rationalism made inroads in three chief areas: the creation of biblical theology, the birth of biblical criticism, and the rise of the modern German university.

The Creation of Biblical Theology

The Enlightenment challenge to confessions continued with Johann Philipp Gabler (1753–1826). If the European philosophical tradition

66. Kant, "What Is Enlightenment?," 19.
67. Kant, "What Is Enlightenment?," 19–20.
68. Kant, "What Is Enlightenment?," 20.
69. Kant, "What Is Enlightenment?," 21.

is a series of footnotes to Plato, as A. N. Whitehead (1861–1947) once observed, then the formal discipline of biblical theology is a footnote to Gabler.[70] Gabler invented biblical theology with his famous inaugural lecture at the University of Altdorf on March 30, 1787, entitled "On the Proper Distinction Between Biblical and Dogmatic Theology and the Specific Objectives of Each." He was concerned about the proliferation of contradictory theological opinions in his day and believed the source of the chaos was "an inappropriate combination of the simplicity and ease of biblical theology with the subtlety and difficulty of dogmatic theology."[71] According to Gabler, biblical theology arises organically from the Bible, whereas theologians create dogmatic theology. One should eliminate dogma, stripping away the accumulated layers of theological opinion to uncover the pristine, eternal religion of the Scriptures. He believed that biblical theologians have to study the Scriptures and determine what therein is truly of divine inspiration and what is merely human opinion.[72] One of the presuppositions of Gabler's method was the inherent superiority of the New Testament over the Old—that the New was the better, and the decidedly *Christian*, testament. He believed that once biblical theologians sifted the biblical text to collect its divinely inspired gems, they then needed to discern what among the collected jewels were truly part of the universal and eternal religion. In this picture, there is no unified, organic, historically unfolding divine revelation in the Scriptures; the Bible only records instances where revelation punctuates history, and even then, one must discriminate among this data to determine what is useful for a chastened dogmatics.[73]

---

70. A. N. Whitehead, *Process and Reality: Corrected Edition*, ed. David Ray Griffin and Donald W. Sherburne (New York: Free Press, 1978), 39; Johann P. Gabler, "An Oration on the Proper Distinction between Biblical and Dogmatic Theology and the Specific Objectives of Each," in *The Flowering of Old Testament Theology: A Reader in Twentieth-Century Old Testament Theology, 1930–1990*, ed. Ben C. Ollenburger, Elmer A. Martens, and Gerhard F. Hasel (Winona Lake, IN: Eisenbrauns, 1992), 489. Note, I say the *formal* discipline; the discipline has materially been a part of the church's hermeneutics for millennia. See J. V. Fesko, "On the Antiquity of Biblical Theology," in *Resurrection and Eschatology: Theology in Service of the Church*, ed. Lane G. Tipton and Jeffrey C. Waddington (Phillipsburg, NJ: P&R, 2008), 443–77.

71. Gabler, "Biblical and Dogmatic Theology," 493.

72. Gabler, "Biblical and Dogmatic Theology," 495–96, 500–501.

73. Gabler, "Biblical and Dogmatic Theology," 501.

Gabler was held captive to the Enlightenment idea that Christianity could be distilled to an essence of universal moral and religious principles. Gabler followed in the footsteps of Johann Semler (1725–91), who argued in his *Treatise on the Free Investigation of the Canon* (1771) that not all parts of the canon are inspired.[74] The litmus test of inspiration is whether the passage under consideration testifies to the universal principles of religion. Both Semler and Gabler were part of the *Neologen* school of thought, which taught that revelation was merely a reaffirmation of moral truths accessible to enlightened reason.[75] Doctrines such as the Trinity and the deity of Christ fell to the wayside because they did not accord with enlightened reason. Kant illustrates the Enlightenment shift from revelation to reason:

> The biblical theologian proves the existence of God on the grounds that He spoke in the Bible, which also discusses His nature (even goes so far into it that reason cannot keep up with the text, as when, for example, it speaks of the incomprehensible mystery of His threefold personality). But the biblical theologian as such cannot and need not prove that God Himself spoke through the Bible, since that is a matter of history and belongs to the philosophy faculty.[76]

As Geerhardus Vos (1862–1949) observed, philosophers and theologians appealed to history in their effort to neutralize claims of divine inspiration.[77] If theologians could not prove inspiration like any other historical fact, then claims of inspiration were discarded as superfluous.

74. Hans Frei, *The Eclipse of Biblical Narrative: A Study of Eighteenth and Nineteenth Century Hermeneutics* (New Haven: Yale University Press, 1980), 111–13; D. A. Carson, "Current Issues in Biblical Theology: A New Testament Perspective," *Bulletin for Biblical Research* 5 (1995): 20.

75. Alister E. McGrath, *The Making of Modern German Christology 1750–1990*, 2nd ed. (Grand Rapids: Zondervan, 1994), 20.

76. Immanuel Kant, *The Conflict of the Faculties*, in *Religion and Rational Theology*, The Cambridge Edition of the Works of Immanuel Kant, ed. and trans. Allen W. Wood and George Di Giovani (Cambridge: Cambridge University Press, 1996), 252.

77. Geerhardus Vos, "The Idea of Biblical Theology as a Science and as a Theological Discipline," in *Redemptive History and Biblical Interpretation: The Shorter Writings of Geerhardus Vos*, ed. Richard B. Gaffin Jr. (Phillipsburg, NJ: Presbyterian and Reformed, 1980), 15.

The Birth of Biblical Criticism

With his essay, Gabler planted a seed that flowered in the development of higher criticism. Michael C. Legaspi aptly captures the Enlightenment shift in the title of his recent book, *The Death of Scripture and the Rise of Biblical Studies*.[78] In the sixteenth and seventeenth centuries, theologians identified theology as the queen of the sciences and philology as merely a handmaiden.[79] But in the earliest phases of the Reformation, scholars (including Erasmus, with his critical edition of the New Testament) paved the way for textual criticism as a formal discipline.[80] After Erasmus, Louis Cappel (1585–1658) published text-critical work on the Old Testament to demonstrate that it was susceptible to change, corruption, and human interference.[81] By the eighteenth century, theologians such as Gabler no longer viewed the Bible as an organically inspired canonical whole but as a disparate collection of texts. Philosophers such as Baruch Spinoza "set aside theological judgments and confessional frameworks for understanding the Bible," which Spinoza regarded as mere opinions and fabrications. Only a historical study of the text of Scripture in accordance with the light of natural reason would protect the reader from errors of ecclesiastical dogmas.[82] Reason, history, and textual criticism would serve as able guides for readers of the Bible.

Kant provides an excellent description of the overall higher-critical methodology in a letter he wrote to a colleague:

> If a religion once reaches the point where critical knowledge of old languages, philological and antiquarian erudition, constitute the foundation on which that religion must be constructed through every age and among all nations, then he who is most at home in Greek,

---

78. Michael C. Legaspi, *The Death of Scripture and the Rise of Biblical Studies* (Oxford: Oxford University Press, 2010).
79. Legaspi, *Death of Scripture*, 11.
80. Legaspi, *Death of Scripture*, 12–13.
81. Legaspi, *Death of Scripture*, 20.
82. Legaspi, *Death of Scripture*, 23; Benedict Spinoza, *Theological-Political Treatise*, ed. Jonathan Israel (Cambridge: Cambridge University Press, 2007), 97–117, 250–59; Steven Nadler, *A Book Forged in Hell: Spinoza's Scandalous Treatise and the Birth of the Secular Age* (Princeton: Princeton University Press, 2011).

Hebrew, Syrian, Arabian etc., and in the archives of antiquity, will drag the orthodox (they may look as sour as they please) like children wherever he wants; they mustn't grumble; for they cannot compare themselves to him in what according to their own confessions carries the power of proof, and they look shyly at a Michaelis as he recasts their ancient treasure in an entirely different coinage. If theological faculties should in time become less insistent on maintaining this sort of literature among their pupils, . . . if philologists independent in their faith should only master this volcanic weapon, then respect for those demagogues will be totally finished and they will have to take instruction from the literary people on what they have to teach.[83]

Systematic theology was no longer queen of the theological sciences; now historical-critical exegesis and philology reigned. Kant believed that philology could irrefutably drag theologians around by their noses and that they could do nothing about it. How could a theologian appeal to the text of Scripture if an enlightened scholar could knock away the load-bearing biblical text through textual criticism or by redefining terminology by appealing to cognate languages and history? Confessions melted under the hot sun of higher criticism.

The Rise of the Modern German University

The third pillar in the Enlightenment challenge to confessions comes in the form of the modern German university. Ideas do not typically captivate an audience apart from an institutional platform. If the printing press and the book publisher were the stage for the Reformation, then the nineteenth-century German university was the rostrum for Enlightenment-driven theology and philosophy. The University of Berlin was founded in 1810, with Friedrich Schleiermacher

83. Immanuel Kant, *Correspondence*, The Cambridge Edition of the Works of Immanuel Kant, trans. and ed. Arnulf Zweig (Cambridge: Cambridge University Press, 1999), 148–49; see Johannes Zachhuber, "The Historical Turn," and David Lincicum, "Criticism and Authority," in *The Oxford Handbook of Nineteenth-Century Christian Thought*, ed. Joel D. S. Rasmussen, Judith Wolfe, and Johannes Zachhuber (Oxford: Oxford University Press, 2017), 53–84, esp. 56. The reference to Michaelis is to Johann David Michaelis (1717–91), a famous orientalist and theologian at Göttingen who cofounded the historical-critical interpretation of the Old Testament (Kant, *Correspondence*, 149n3; Legaspi, *Death of Scripture*, 33–37).

(1768–1834) as its chief intellectual architect.[84] Studying theology at a university was not uncommon, as theologians had done this for centuries. Schleiermacher and the founders of the University of Berlin, however, were very specific about how theology would be studied in this new academic setting. In line with Kant's understanding of enlightenment, professors at the University of Berlin believed that theology had to be studied as a science (*Wissenschaft*), and the only way to undertake the truly scientific study of the Scriptures was to sever it from the church. Studying theology under the auspices of the church was positively injurious to true *Wissenschaft*. Only when theology was released from the confessional bonds of the church could it flourish and contribute to the edifice of modern science and culture.[85] With Kant, Schleiermacher believed that the philosophy faculty was lord over the other faculties, including theology. Only a dispassionate, scientific study of the Scriptures—*Wissenschaft* for its own sake, apart from practical or professional interests—could be of true benefit to society.[86] In line with Kant's description of enlightenment, through critical, scientific inquiry, theologians were supposed to excise the diseased and weakened forms of Christianity and steer the church toward a closer approximation of pure religion.[87]

A second factor further separated church and confessions from the study of theology—namely, the structure of the theological curriculum. Schleiermacher introduced his *Brief Outline on the Study of Theology* (1811) as the charter for the theological curriculum at the university.[88] Schleiermacher formally subdivided the curriculum into three departments: philosophical, practical, and historical theology.[89] In some respects this division mirrored early modern methods for studying the Scriptures formalized by Andreas

---

84. Thomas Albert Howard, *Protestant Theology and the Making of the Modern German University* (Oxford: Oxford University Press, 2006), 8–9.

85. Howard, *Protestant Theology*, 15.

86. Howard, *Protestant Theology*, 167–68.

87. Howard, *Protestant Theology*, 205.

88. Howard, *Protestant Theology*, 133; Friedrich Schleiermacher, *Brief Outline on the Study of Theology*, trans. Terrence N. Tice (Richmond: John Knox, 1966). For a study on the impact of the Enlightenment on the study of theology, see Zachary Purvis, *Theology and the University in Nineteenth-Century Germany* (Oxford: Oxford University Press, 2016).

89. Schleiermacher, *Outline*, 25–27.

Hyperius (1511–64): biblical exegesis, dogmatics, church history, and practical theology.[90] Even though there are similarities between the two methods, their respective contexts create very different outcomes. In the premodern study of the Scriptures, theologians did not seek scientific knowledge (*Wissenschaft* or *scientia*) but wisdom (*sapientia*). There are two correlates of this ethos: (1) premodern theologians recognized that the ecclesial context was necessary for the study of the Scriptures, and (2) they believed that the spiritual well-being of the theologians who studied the Scriptures was paramount.[91]

Luther, for example, argues that the three most important rules for the study of the Scriptures are prayer (*oratio*), meditation (*meditatio*), and testing (*tentatio*). First one must pray, because only the Spirit illumines the Scriptures to the sin-darkened mind; the Spirit must strengthen one's faith. Meditation is necessary because a theologian needs to inscribe the Word of God on his or her heart and mind, and so the student of Scripture must read, reread, and reflect. Testing (in German, *Anfechtung*) is necessary because, apart from adversity, bare knowledge is insufficient when only a personal experience of God's love and mercy will do.[92] In short, the study of theology was more than an intellectual exercise; rather, it was a holistic experience aimed at two goals: conforming the Christian to the image of God and learning, loving, and longing for the one who stands behind the Scriptures.[93]

Architecture illustrates the shift in the study of the Scriptures that took place in the modern era. No longer did theologians study the Bible in monasteries, churches, and Gothic cathedrals. Rather, the study of the Scriptures was now conducted in secular universities that purposefully severed the link between church and academy. A serious student of the Scriptures was no longer a minister of the gospel who lectured, preached, and served within the context of the church and for the church but an academic scholar studying a scientific discipline,

---

90. Howard, *Protestant Theology*, 76.
91. Howard, *Protestant Theology*, 16–17.
92. Howard, *Protestant Theology*, 72.
93. Ellen T. Charry, *By the Renewing of Your Minds: The Pastoral Function of Christian Doctrine* (Oxford: Oxford University Press, 1997).

which was an end unto itself. In this context Schleiermacher's tri-partite curricular division fostered the splintering of the theological disciplines. Moses was not the author of the Pentateuch, and the prophets were not the guardians of Yahweh's inspired revelation that had its telos in Christ, the God-man. The Pentateuch was a disparate collection of human texts gathered together by ham-fisted editors, and the prophets were poetic geniuses who did not defend the inspired Word of God but "the ruins of a dismantled canon shrouded in the mist of a venerable Hebraic past."[94]

In his reflections on original sin, poet, philosopher, and theologian Samuel Taylor Coleridge (1772–1834) describes the impact of severing the church from the academy:

> Where the mysteries of religion, and truths supersensual, are either cut and squared for the comprehension of the Understanding, the faculty judging according to sense, or desperately torn asunder from the Reason, nay fanatically opposed to it; lastly, where private interpretation is every thing, and the Church nothing—there the mystery of Original Sin will be either rejected, or evaded, or perverted into the monstrous fiction of hereditary sin,—guilt inherited; in the mystery of Redemption metaphors will be obtruded for the reality; and in the mysterious appurtenants and symbols of Redemption (regeneration, grace, the Eucharist, and spiritual communion) the realities will be evaporated into metaphors.[95]

Shorn from its ecclesial and confessional anchor, the scientific study of theology was free to drift wherever the winds of reason took it. The theology faculty of the modern German university was no longer under the church and therefore had no need for confessions.

Mysticism and Pietism

Schleiermacher and Mysticism

Many Christians felt the weight of higher critical study of the Scriptures and saw long-standing doctrines seemingly razed. A com-

94. Legaspi, *Death of Scripture*, 128.
95. Samuel Taylor Coleridge, *Aphorisms on That Which Is Indeed Spiritual Religion*, in *The Complete Works of Samuel Taylor Coleridge*, ed. W. G. T. Shedd, 7 vols. (New York: Harper & Brothers, 1863), 1:294–95; Legaspi, *Death of Scripture*, 105.

mon response to this trend was to retreat to mysticism and the inner confines of the soul, far out of reach of the scientific claims about the Bible. Ironically, Schleiermacher was one of the chief driving forces behind the turn to mysticism with his promotion of the idea of *das schlechthinnige abhängigkeitsgefühl* (the feeling of absolute dependence). Schleiermacher was not entirely committed to Kant's rationalism. He wanted to leave room for faith:

> Religion does not strive to bring those who believe and feel under a single belief and a single feeling. It strives, to be sure, to open the eyes of those who are not yet capable of intuiting the universe, for every one who sees is a new priest, a new mediator, a new mouthpiece; but for just this reason it avoids with aversion the barren uniformity that would again destroy the divine abundance.[96]

This statement reveals an anticonfessional bent—as a "single belief," if mandated, would stifle the divine abundance in its variegated manifestations to different people. Schleiermacher prioritized the individual's subjective state over the authority of Scripture. Schleiermacher's tome on Christian doctrine, known as the *Glaubenslehre* (that is, the "doctrine *of faith*" rather than *of theology*, the study of God), reveals this shift in priority from the objective to the subjective.[97]

Lutheran Pietism

Enlightenment mysticism arguably has some roots in the earlier pietist movement launched by Philip Jacob Spener (1635–1705), otherwise known as the father of pietism. Spener labored in the wake of the destructive Thirty Years' War, and interconfessional polemics was therefore a significant factor in the formation of his

96. Friedrich Schleiermacher, *On Religion: Speeches to Its Cultured Despisers*, trans. and ed. Richard Crouter (Cambridge: Cambridge University Press, 1996), 28.
97. For the definitive English critical edition, see Friedrich Schleiermacher, *Christian Faith: A New Translation and Critical Edition*, trans. Edwina Lawler, trans. and ed. Terrence N. Tice and Catherine L. Kelsey, 2 vols. (Louisville: Westminster John Knox, 2016); see also Schleiermacher, *Der christliche Glaube nach den Grundsätzen der evangelischen Kirche. Glaubenslehre in 4 Bänden*, Bibliothek theologischer Klassiker Bde. 13–16 (Gotha: Perthes, 1889).

views.[98] Spener believed that there was a lack of piety in the Lutheran church and so wrote his *Pia Desideria* (*Pious Desires*), which expressed his craving for reform. Spener described the church as being in a state of distress and sickness.[99] In particular, he believed that the clergy of the Lutheran church were corrupt. Ministers were guilty of scandal, vices, and immorality. Ministers were only interested in moving from parish to parish as they climbed the ecclesial ladder of success.[100] Spener describes the wayward ministers in the following manner:

> To be sure, as others have acquired knowledge in their fields of study, so these preachers, with their own human efforts and without the working of the Holy Spirt, have learned something of the letter of the Scriptures, have comprehended and assented to true doctrine, and have even known how to preach it to others, but they are altogether unacquainted with the true, heavenly light and the life of faith.[101]

Spener does not deride or complain about confessions or doctrinal orthodoxy; he laments that ministers do not practice what they have learned. In fact, Spener approvingly cites similar observations by some of the Lutheran tradition's greatest scholastic theologians, including Johann Gerhard (1582–1637) and David Chytraeus (1530–1600).[102] Chytraeus was one of the authors of the Formula of Concord (1577), and thus not averse to confessions, but he also saw the need for piety: "The study of theology should be carried on not by the strife of disputations but rather by the practice of piety."[103]

Spener's complaint, therefore, was not against confessions or scholastic orthodoxy per se; rather, it was against impious ministers and theologians. He believed they were enchanted by the subtleties of

98. Theodore G. Tappert, introduction to *Pia Desideria*, by Philip Jacob Spener, ed. Theodore G. Tappert (Philadelphia: Fortress, 1964), 5.
99. Spener, *Pia Desideria*, 31, 42.
100. Spener, *Pia Desideria*, 44–45.
101. Spener, *Pia Desideria*, 46.
102. Spener, *Pia Desideria*, 48, 50.
103. David Chytraeus, *Oratio de Studio Theologiae Recte Inchoando* 20, as cited in Spener, *Pia Desideria*, 50.

doctrine and the siren call of reason rather than by the simplicity of the Scriptures:

> When they really achieve the purpose they set themselves, they succeed in giving those of their hearers who have ready minds a fair knowledge of religious controversies, and these hearers regard it as the greatest honor to dispute with others. Both preachers and hearers confine themselves to the notion that the one thing needful is the assertion and retention of pure doctrine, which must not be overthrown by errors, even if it is very much obscured with human perversions.[104]

Again, Spener's concern is with overly truculent ministers always ready to debate doctrine and ensure that it is pure but who deface this orthodoxy with immorality and vice. This inattention to piety flowed out of pulpits into the pews and was manifest in drunkenness, litigiousness, and other moral failings in the church.[105] Another consequence of ministerial impiety was that Roman Catholics who wanted to leave due to the Catholic Church's false doctrine would not come to the Lutheran church because of its apparent immorality. Spener labels Rome as "heterodox" and commends Lutheran doctrine as orthodox, though obscured by a cloud of impiety.[106]

Spener proposed six remedies to reform the Lutheran church. First, he wanted to see the Word of God used extensively in the church.[107] Spener did not object to catechetical sermons, but he wanted to ensure that they rested in the authority of the Scriptures. He encouraged the private devotional use of the Scriptures.[108] His idea that people start house churches led by knowledgeable members under the supervision of ministers was likely controversial.[109] Second, he proposed the diligent exercise of spiritual priesthood.[110] Since all believers share in the priesthood of Christ, he believed all Christians should maximize their priestly status. Rather than reserve the serious study of the Scriptures

104. Spener, *Pia Desideria*, 56.
105. Spener, *Pia Desideria*, 57–68.
106. Spener, *Pia Desideria*, 70–71.
107. Spener, *Pia Desideria*, 87.
108. Spener, *Pia Desideria*, 89.
109. Spener, *Pia Desideria*, 89.
110. Spener, *Pia Desideria*, 92.

for the clergy, Spener wanted lay Christians to delve into the Bible. An ignorant laity was the way that Rome held the church in check, and he didn't want the same thing to happen in Protestant churches.[111] Third, Spener insisted that Christians adorn their doctrinal knowledge with practice.[112] Fourth, Christians had to guard their piety while engaging in religious controversies.[113] Christians were supposed to lead others away from doctrinal error but in a loving and charitable manner.[114] Spener was embarrassed by Luther's violent and coarse language in disputes.[115] In some cases, Spener believed that Christians should steer clear of disputes (not all controversies are worthy of engagement).[116] Fifth, since ministers were the primary means by which these reforms would occur, Spener suggested that only godly men should serve as pastors. They should be trained in schools and universities, but professors should ensure that these institutions are not places of "ambition, tippling, carousing, and brawling."[117] Rather, they should foster godly conduct.

In support of this claim, Spener again appeals to a Lutheran scholastic theologian, this time Abraham Calovius (1612–86). Calovius published many books in defense of orthodoxy, but he also stressed the need for holiness of life.[118] To bring about this wedding of doctrine and piety, Spener encouraged professors to model it for their students and to hold them accountable if they saw their students engaging in "riotous living, tippling, bragging, and boasting of academic and other preeminence."[119] Another way of encouraging students to greater piety was to have professors commend certain works, such as *The Imitation of Christ* by Thomas à Kempis (ca. 1380–1471) and the *Theologica Germanica*—medieval books that promoted mysticism.[120]

111. Spener, *Pia Desideria*, 93–94.
112. Spener, *Pia Desideria*, 95.
113. Spener, *Pia Desideria*, 97.
114. Spener, *Pia Desideria*, 9–99.
115. K. James Stein, "Philipp Jakob Spener," in *The Pietist Theologians: An Introduction to Theology in the Seventeenth and Eighteenth Century*, ed. Carter Lindberg (Oxford: Blackwell, 2005), 85.
116. Spener, *Pia Desideria*, 100.
117. Spener, *Pia Desideria*, 103.
118. Spener, *Pia Desideria*, 105–6.
119. Spener, *Pia Desideria*, 107.
120. Spener, *Pia Desideria*, 110–11.

Spener was well aware that the "darkness of their age" still clung to these works, but he believed that the discerning reader could strain out the problematic elements and still benefit from them.[121] As his sixth and finally remedy, Spener wanted better preaching. Rather than rhetoric and presentation, he thought preachers should focus on content that the average person could comprehend.[122]

Spener's *Pia Desideria* is important for at least two reasons. First, a close examination of the work reveals that Spener was not opposed to scholasticism, orthodoxy, confessions, or catechisms. Yet this is precisely how some historians characterize Spener's work. In his introduction to Spener's treatise, Theodore Tappert claims that theologians in Spener's day taught an inherited theology that was reduced to compendiums infected with Aristotle's philosophy. Tappert writes, "Independent exegesis of the Scriptures had little place in the curriculum at a time when it was assumed that the contents of the Scriptures were adequately expressed in the Confessions. The want of a historical understanding of the past, even of the Reformation, contributed to the tendency to look upon theological statements as timeless truths and to identify the Christian faith with intellectual propositions."[123] Yet Spener says nothing of the sort. In fact, in his treatise he approvingly cites numerous defenders of Lutheran confessional orthodoxy such as Gerhard, Calovius, and Chytraeus. Likewise, John Frame claims, "Theological orthodoxy had a deadening effect on the practical Christian life."[124] Yet Frame does not demonstrate the supposed connection between confessional orthodoxy and antinomianism. The same narrative appears in the introduction to the works of Valentin Ernst Löscher (1673–1749), where the editors pit "subjectivism versus orthodox doctrine, or emotionalism versus Confessionalism."[125] Spener's work does not assume this connection; in fact, he sees confessions and piety as compatible (as his ardent

---

121. Spener, *Pia Desideria*, 112.
122. Spener, *Pia Desideria*, 115–16.
123. Tappert, "Introduction," 5–6.
124. John Frame, *A History of Western Philosophy and Theology* (Phillipsburg, NJ: P&R, 2015), 176.
125. Timothy M. Salo, "Joachim Lange: Lutheran Pietist Theologian and Halle Apologist," in *The Pietist Impulse in Christianity*, ed. Christian T. Collins Winn et al. (London: James Clarke, 2011), 87; Valentin Ernst Löscher, *The Complete Timotheus*

catechetical labors reveal). He also polemicized against Roman Catholic and Socinian doctrine and expressed his disagreement with Reformed theologians over typically debated issues, including predestination, Christology, and the Lord's Supper.[126] For Spener, the defect lies not with the confessions but with the people who profess them, as the different sections of his treatise reveal; it lies with the magistrates, the clergy, and the common people.

Second, even though Spener did not take issue with confessions or with Lutheran orthodoxy, elements of his proposal arguably did sow the seeds of individualism and mysticism. Encouraging small groups of individuals to study the Scriptures, to teach them, and to express their doubts about them could undermine the corporate faith of the church.[127] Recommending mystical works such as the *Theologica Germanica* and *The Imitation of Christ* promoted a mysticism devoid of Scripture and contributed to confessional erosion that eventually severed the church and academy at the University of Berlin. Ironically, Westminster divine Samuel Rutherford was critical of the *Theologica Germanica* because he believed it incited antinomianism and was a significant influence on Anabaptist theologians such as Hans Denck (ca. 1495–1527).[128] The *Theologica Germanica* taught perfectionism; believers could eventually shed the need for the moral law. This work was also influential among a number of English antinomian sects.[129] In fact, when orthodox Lutheran Valentin Löscher challenged pietist theologians, he criticized them for their contempt for the ordinary means of grace in the sacraments.[130]

One can summarize Spener's critique as a debate among confessional Lutheran theologians regarding how best to pursue the Chris-

Verinus, trans. James Langebartels and Robert J. Koester (Milwaukee: Northwestern Publishing, 1998), v–ix; see also Stein, "Philipp Jakob Spener," 86, 88–89, 96.

126. Stein, "Philipp Jakob Spener," 84–85.

127. Stein, "Philipp Jakob Spener," 87–89.

128. Samuel Rutherford, *A Survey of the Spiritual Antichrist* 1.14, 2.84 (London, 1648), 163, 193; see Martin Luther, *The Theologia Germanica of Martin Luther*, trans. Susanna Winkworth (Mineola, NY: Dover Publications, 2004).

129. David R. Como, *Blown by the Spirit: Puritanism and the Emergence of an Antinomian Underground in Pre–Civil-War England* (Stanford, CA: Stanford University Press, 2004), 39.

130. Löscher, *Complete Timotheus Verinus*, 63–92.

tian life. Nevertheless, certain pietist emphases contributed to the eventual rejection of church authority and confessions. As different as pietism is from rationalism, the two have often worked together to undermine confessionalism. As B. B. Warfield (1851–1921) once observed, "Extremes meet. Pietist and Rationalist have ever hunted in couples and dragged down their quarry together. They may differ as to why they deem theology mere lumber, and would not have the prospective minister waste his time in acquiring it. The one loves God so much, the other loves him so little, that he does not care to know him. But they agree that it is not worth while to learn to know him."[131]

Individualism

Many theologians and philosophers have described the present day as the dawn of the postmodern age, a new era in Western philosophical thought. For example, Stanley Grenz (1950–2005) and John Franke claim, "Theology is in a time of transition and ferment, partly as a result of the collapse of the categories and paradigms of the modern world as spawned by the Enlightenment."[132] It is said that we live no longer in the modern world but, rather, in the postmodern world. That said, some believe postmodernity is on its way out because it was inherently temporary, a kind of ferry to transport Western culture from modernity to an as-yet-unknown philosophical destination.[133] But as tempting as it might be to characterize the present day as a new development in the unfolding narrative of Western philosophy, we have to ask whether we truly live in a *postmodern* context or, rather, in a *hypermodern* one. I would contend that we do not live in a period in which people apply new categories of thought, thus meriting the prefix *post-* to signal that the world has moved beyond modernity. Rather, all of the aforementioned forces contributing to

131. B. B. Warfield, "Our Seminary Curriculum," in *Benjamin B. Warfield: Selected Shorter Writings*, ed. John E. Meeter, 2 vols. (Phillipsburg, NJ: P&R, 2001), 1:371.

132. Stanley J. Grenz and John R. Franke, *Beyond Foundationalism: Shaping Theology in a Postmodern Context* (Louisville: Westminster John Knox, 2001), 3.

133. Umberto Eco, *Chronicles of a Liquid Society* (Boston: Houghton Mifflin Harcourt, 2017), 1.

the rejection of confessionalism still persist: skepticism, the push for religious freedom and toleration, Lockean individualism, Kantian notions of rational autonomy, the divorce of biblical and systematic theology, higher critical views of Scripture, the separation of the church and the academy, pietism, and mysticism. We live not in a postmodern period but rather in a hypermodern age.[134] That is, all of these forces exist in exacerbated form. These different developments have given birth to the dominant religion of the enlightened West—namely, Moralistic Therapeutic Deism.[135]

One might characterize the present day as Kantian autonomy mixed with heavy doses of skepticism and mysticism. But what makes this potion so potent is the steroid of technological consumerism. Unlike past ages, when limited economic and material resources prevented people from engaging in mass consumption, the present day has no such limitations. People move from one act of consumption to another, gorging wastefully and without purpose. The new technological gadget is only marginally better than the old, but the old must be tossed aside in order to gratify appetites that have long since gone off the rails.[136] Unbridled consumption, autonomy, mysticism, and skepticism have created a crisis in which the concept of community gives way to unbridled individualism. As Umberto Eco (1932–2016) observed, "People are no longer fellow citizens, but rivals to beware of."[137] In this period of hypermodernity, community identities are collapsing under the weight of a narcissistic idealism.[138] Aided by technology, individuals can apply Kantian idealism with a vengeance and shape reality to suit their personal preferences—that is, they can create a virtual reality. Eco describes this scenario as the "liquefica-

134. See J. Richard Middleton and Brian J. Walsh, *Truth Is Stranger Than It Used to Be: Biblical Faith in a Postmodern Age* (Downers Grove, IL: InterVarsity, 1996), 41–42.

135. Christian Smith with Melinda Lundquist Denton, *Soul Searching: The Religious and Spiritual Lives of American Teenagers* (Oxford: Oxford University Press, 2005), 162–70.

136. Eco, *Liquid Society*, 2.

137. Eco, *Liquid Society*, 2.

138. On the current narcissistic culture, see Jean M. Twenge and W. Keith Campbell, *The Narcissism Epidemic: Living in the Age of Entitlement* (New York: Free Press, 2010); Christopher Lasch, *The Culture of Narcissism: American Life in an Age of Diminishing Expectations* (New York: Norton, 1979).

tion" of society; everything is fluid.[139] But he also notes that only indignation is left "once faith in salvation from above, from the state, or from revolution is gone." People know what they reject but have no idea what they truly want.[140] In such a context, the same cultural and philosophical forces that worked against confessionalism in the modern age remain and show no sign of abatement.

Conclusion

From this survey of the case against confessions, we can make at least three observations. First, part of the blame for the collapse of confessionalism lies within the church itself. In the early modern period, the connection between theological controversy and bloodshed is undeniable. The Reformed theologians were children of their times and thus did not conduct themselves any differently in these controversies than their Roman Catholic peers. Confessions were enforced and promoted by means of the sword, and that fact proved devastating both to confessionalism and to Western Europe. Blame for the collapse of confessionalism also rests on theologians who were lax in the practice of church discipline with the morally wayward, which led Pietists to seek solutions in medieval mystical works such as the *Theologica Germanica* and à Kempis's *The Imitation of Christ*. And so, theologically inspired violence, failures in church discipline, and mysticism weakened confessionalism from within. Second, Enlightenment notions of autonomy, skepticism, and mysticism weakened confessionalism from without. Plain and simple, nominal Christians poured the acid of unbelief on the confessions of the church. Third, despite all of the claims that we have been moving past the categories of modernity, not much has changed. The various corrosive trends (autonomy, skepticism, mysticism) have waxed and waned over the last four centuries, but they have always been present to one degree or another. Confessional churches need to learn from their past errors while still authentically professing the faith once delivered to the saints and passed down through their creeds, confessions, and catechisms.

139. Eco, *Liquid Society*, 2.
140. Eco, *Liquid Society*, 2.

FOUR

Benefits of Confessions

Introduction

In the hyperindividualistic age in which we live, writing about the advantages of creeds and confessions might seem like the ultimate Quixotic adventure. Don Quixote lived in a world that had long-since moved beyond knights and chivalry; people thought he was a fool trying to live in the past. In a world that has moved beyond confessions, does not the quest to identify the benefits of confessions amount to little more than trying to turn back the clock and return to a bygone era? As out of place as it might seem, the present antipathy toward confessions might characterize a majority of evangelical Christians, but in the broader scope of the last two thousand years, confessionalism is most certainly the majority report. The overwhelming majority of the church has employed creeds and confessions over the last two thousand years, and for many good reasons—reasons that still apply today. This chapter, however, focuses on just three benefits. It advances the thesis that creeds and confessions are beneficial for the church because they (1) distinguish orthodoxy from heterodoxy, (2) create boundaries that foster a diversified orthodoxy, and (3) codify the church's historic witness.[1]

1. For other benefits, see Carl R. Trueman, *The Creedal Imperative* (Wheaton: Crossway, 2012), 159–85.

In other words, confessions assist the church in distinguishing truth from falsehood. The church does not merely repeat the words of the Bible; it must interpret the Bible. Not all interpretations are valid or true. Confessions set boundaries. But within these defined parameters, the best confessions allow for an ecclesiastically defined diversity of opinion on various issues. Confessions also encourage the church today to take account of the church throughout the ages. In the words of G. K. Chesterton (1874–1936), confessions encourage the church to exercise a "democracy of the dead": when considering important truths, the church must not merely consult those who are alive; it must also seek the opinions of those who have gone before.[2]

Distinguishing Orthodoxy from Heterodoxy

One of the greatest benefits of creeds and confessions is that they draw a line between orthodoxy and heterodoxy. As noted in chapter 1, confessing the faith is not merely an exercise in repeating biblical statements. The church has the responsibility of repeating, meditating on, and interpreting biblical claims in harmony with divine authorial intent. In Paul's letter to the Galatians, we hear that false teachers claimed fidelity to the gospel of Christ. They preached Christ and instructed the Galatians in the faith. Yet Paul clearly identifies their teaching as "a different gospel" (Gal. 1:6). The Judaizers were distorting the gospel, so Paul levels his anathemas against any angel or human who preaches another message (Gal. 1:8–9). The church always needs to discern the difference between truth and falsehood. There are numerous examples of this discernment process throughout the Scriptures: Elijah faces the prophets of Baal (1 Kings 18:20–40); Paul, as we have seen, opposes the Judaizers in Galatia; and John engages docetists (1 John 4:2–3; 2 John 7). As David Steinmetz (1936–2015) observes,

> A myriad of quotations from the Bible does not make the arguments of the theologian who quotes it biblical. Heretics are like witty guests

2. G. K. Chesterton, *Orthodoxy: The Romance of Faith* (1908; repr., New York: Doubleday, 1990), 48.

who entertain at parties by spontaneously constructing new poems from old. They quote well-loved lines from the works of established poets. Every line in the new poem is from Virgil or Horace and yet Virgil and Horace did not write it. The words are from the original poet, but the architectonic structure is not. Heretics, lost in the sprawling narrative of the Bible and ignorant of the second narrative that ties it together, have constructed a second narrative of their own. The words are from the Bible, but what the words say is not biblical.[3]

One must demarcate legitimate from illegitimate uses of the Bible. Confessions of faith perform this very function.

Throughout their confession, the Westminster divines provide boundaries that serve this purpose. The opening paragraph of the eleventh chapter (on justification) is an excellent example:

> Those whom God effectually calleth, he also freely justifieth: not, by infusing righteousnesse into them, but by pardoning their sins, and by accounting and accepting their persons as righteous; not, for any thing wrought in them, or done by them, but for Christs sake alone; nor, by imputing faith it self, the act of beleeving, or any other evangelicall obedience, to them, as their righteousnesse, but, by imputing the obedience and satisfaction of Christ unto them, they receiving, and resting on him and his righteousnesse by faith; which faith, they have, not of themselves, it is the gift of God.[4]

This statement echoes a number of biblical passages and concepts such as calling, justification, imputation, faith, and righteousness. The paragraph also alludes to the closing words of Ephesians 2:8–9: "For by grace you have been saved through faith. And this is not your own doing; it is the gift of God, not a result of works, so that no one may boast." In some respects, the divines offer nothing unique in comparison with Roman Catholic or Remonstrant statements on justification.[5]

---

3. David Steinmetz, *Taking the Long View: Christian Theology in Historical Perspective* (Oxford: Oxford University Press, 2011), 18.

4. *The Humble Advice of the Assembly of Divines, Now by Authority of Parliament Sitting at Westminster, Concerning a Confession of Faith* (London, 1647), 11.1.

5. Council of Trent, "Decree on Justification," Session 6, 13 January 1547, in *Creeds and Confessions of Faith in the Christian Tradition*, ed. Jaroslav Pelikan and Valerie Hotchkiss, 4 vols. (New Haven: Yale University Press, 2003), 2:826–39;

Yet three qualifications distinguish Westminster from Roman Catholic and Remonstrant confessions on this doctrine.

First, the divines say that justification is not by the infusion of righteousness into the believer; rather, it is God's pardoning of sin and counting and accepting persons as righteous. This is a direct refutation of Roman Catholic views—which claimed that God infuses the gifts of charity into the soul through baptism (in an initial justification) but that believers must then exercise faith working through love in order to secure their final justification.[6] In contrast to this Roman Catholic view, the divines explain that justification consists in the forgiveness of sins and the imputation of Christ's righteousness.

The second qualification appears when they say that justification is not "for any thing wrought in them, or done by them, but for Christs sake alone." This statement is a continuation of the first stipulation, as infused righteousness and faith working through love go hand in hand. But to be sure—in case one might reject infused righteousness while still claiming that justification somehow rests either in the believer's union with Christ, as in the views of Andreas Osiander (1498–1552), or in the believer's good works, as in Roman Catholicism—the divines close this path.[7]

The third qualification is that, according to the Westminster divines, justification is not a result of "imputing faith it self, the act of beleeving, or any other evangelicall obedience, to them, as their righteousnesse." The divines chiefly had the views of Jacob Arminius

---

Mark A. Ellis, trans. and ed., *The Arminian Confession of 1621* (Eugene, OR: Wipf & Stock, 2005), chap. 11 (pp. 78–82). Unless otherwise noted, quotations and citations of confessional documents come from Pelikan and Hotchkiss.

6. Council of Trent, "Decree on Justification," chap. 10 (Pelikan and Hotchkiss, 2:831); Robert Bellarmine, *De Iustificatione Impii Libri Quinque* 4.18, in *Disputationum Roberti Bellarmini* (Naples, 1858), 593–97; John W. O'Malley, *Trent: What Happened at the Council* (Cambridge, MA: Belknap, 2013), 102–16; Hubert Jedin, *Papal Legate at the Council of Trent: Cardinal Seripando* (St. Louis: B. Herder Book Co., 1947), 326–92; Jedin, *A History of the Council of Trent*, 2 vols. (London: Thomas Nelson and Sons, 1963), 166–96.

7. Andreas Osiander, *Disputatio de Iustificatione (1550)*, in *Gesamtausgabe*, vol. 9 (Gütersloh: Gütersloh Verlagshaus, 1994), 422–47; Timothy J. Wengert, *Defending the Faith: Lutheran Responses to Andreas Osiander's Doctrine of Justification, 1551–59* (Tübingen: Mohr Siebeck, 2012).

(1560–1609) in their crosshairs with this clarification.[8] Arminius rejected the common Reformed view regarding Romans 4:3, "Abraham believed God, and it was counted to him as righteousness."[9] Reformed exegetes typically argued that when Paul wrote that God counted Abraham's faith as righteousness, he used the term *faith* (πίστις) or *believe* (πιστεύω) metonymically.[10] A metonym is when an author uses a word for one object as a reference to another object. In the phrase "today the Pentagon announced," *Pentagon* is a metonym for the Department of Defense. The physical building of the Pentagon is incapable of making statements but serves as a reference to the governmental department that issued the statement. The common Reformed view on Romans 4:3, then, was that when Paul writes of Abraham's faith, he has Christ's righteousness as the intended referent. Arminius, on the other hand, believed that Paul was not referring to Christ's righteousness but to Abraham's personal faith. In his view, God looked upon Abraham's faith as if it were righteousness.

In other words, for Arminius, the believer's justification rests in his or her faith, whereas for the Westminster divines, faith is an instrument that lays hold of the satisfaction and righteousness of Christ. For Arminius, faith is foundational for justification, whereas for Westminster, it is instrumental. One of the Westminster divines zeroed in on Arminius's view and rejected it. George Walker (ca. 1581–1651) writes that Arminius

> did first secretly teach and instill it into the ears and hearts of many disciples; and afterwards did openly professe it, as we read in his Epistle *ad Hyppolytum de collibus*, wherein he confesseth that he held, faith to be imputed for righteousnesse to justification, not in a metonymicall, but in a proper sense: And although this and other

8. For an overview of Arminius's doctrine of justification, see J. V. Fesko, "Arminius on Justification: Reformed or Protestant?," *Church History and Religious Culture* 94 (2014): 1–21.

9. Jacob Arminius, "Letter to Hippolytus à Collibus, 8 April 1608," sect. 5, in *The Works of James Arminius*, trans. James Nichols and William Nichols, 3 vols. (Grand Rapids: Baker, 1986), 2:702.

10. See, e.g., Johannes Wollebius, *Compendium Theologiae Christianae*, in *Reformed Dogmatics*, ed. John W. Beardslee (Oxford: Oxford University Press, 1965), 165; Girolamo Zanchi, *De Religione Christiana Fides—Confession of Christian Religion* 19.6, ed. Luca Baschera and Christian Moser (Leiden: Brill, 2007), 1:342–43.

errours held by him are condemned in the late Synod of Dort: yet
his disciples the Remonstrants doe obstinately persist in this errour,
though some of that sect, would seem to decline and disclaime it.[11]

Thus, in this one paragraph the divines define justification but offer three
interpretive qualifications as to both what it is and what it is not. They
distinguish orthodoxy from heterodoxy with razor-sharp precision.

Creating a Diversified Orthodoxy

One common fear about confessions is that, in the drive to demarcate
the boundaries of orthodoxy, the confessional church will soon find
itself wearing the straitjacket of fundamentalism, and that fundamentalism will quickly lead to violence. For example, Harvey Cox
(1929–) claims that, in the wake of Constantine's conversion, "Christian imperial authorities put twenty-five thousand to death for their
lack of creedal correctness."[12] For Cox, Christianity is neither a creed
nor a set of axioms but a faith for embodiment.[13] He dispenses with
theological fences because he believes that the Bible presents only
one of many different ways to perceive the mystery of the universe.[14]
Confessions are nothing more to him than historical landmarks to
remind people what the church has historically professed; they cannot
serve as doctrinal bulwarks. He believes the church needs a second
Reformation, but one based on deeds rather than creeds.[15]

On the one hand, Cox has a point. The previous chapter noted
that bloodshed along confessional lines is among the reasons for the
demise of confessionalism. At the same time, American Presbyterians
made the necessary doctrinal correctives to the Westminster Standards to ensure that the sword stays far out of the church's reach.[16]

11. George Walker, *Socinianisme in the Fundamental Point of Justification Discovered and Confuted* (London, 1641), 5–6.
12. Harvey Cox, *The Future of Faith* (San Francisco: HarperOne, 2009), 7.
13. Cox, *Future of Faith*, 19.
14. Cox, *Future of Faith*, 41.
15. Cox, *Future of Faith*, 76.
16. D. G. Hart and John R. Muether, *Seeking a Better Country: 300 Years of
American Presbyterianism* (Phillipsburg, NJ: P&R, 2007), 82–88.

And unlike Rome, the Reformed churches have never claimed doctrinal infallibility for their creeds, confessions, and catechisms. Rather, the Reformed churches acknowledge in their creedal documents the supremacy of the authority of Scripture and that all of their confessional documents are subject to revision.[17]

The Westminster divines were certainly concerned to secure numerous doctrines through precise statements, such as the above-surveyed statement on justification. Other such detailed expositions of doctrine include the Westminster Confession's chapters on the decree (3) and the Lord's Supper (29). At the same time, the divines were equally concerned to write confessional passages marked by deliberate ambiguity to facilitate a diversified orthodoxy. Three examples in the confession illustrate this—its chapters on the decree (3), the covenants (7), and assurance (18).

Within the assembly, there were differing opinions regarding the nature of the divine decree(s). Yet, while the divines had their convictions about these matters, they also recognized that they were treading on holy ground. They knew that the closer they sought to draw to God's mind on the subject, the more the light of his glory would blind their feeble minds. They were therefore quite circumspect about the subject and wanted to ensure that they stated only what was confessionally necessary, not what was maximally possible. During the assembly's deliberations, scribes captured some of the dialogue.

Samuel Rutherford (ca. 1600–1661) saw both agreement and disagreement: all agreed that God decrees the end and the means of every event, but opinions differed over whether there were multiple divine decrees or a single decree. Rutherford was content to say "God also hath decreed," but he did not want the assembly to decide the question of whether there was only one decree or whether there were multiple. He did not believe that such an opinion was suitable for a confession of faith. Edward Reynolds (1599–1676) acknowledged that the assembly's prolocutor, William Twisse (1578–1646), had written extensively on the subject and thus had certain opinions on the matter, but Reynolds too thought it inadvisable for inclusion in a confession of faith. George Gillespie (1613–48) believed that this was a prudent

---

17. *Westminster Confession of Faith*, 1.10.

course of action and favored excluding reference to the specific issue; by eliminating the issue from the confession, he proclaimed, "Every one may enjoy his own sense."[18] In fact, to capture the diversity of opinion, the standards oscillate back and forth between the terms *decree* (as in 3.3, 5.2, 11.4, and 17.2 of the Confession and questions 13 and 79 of the Larger Catechism) and *decrees* (as in questions 6, 12, 14, and 113 of the Larger Catechism).[19] In other words, bypassing the question regarding the number of decrees allowed each member of the assembly to hold his own opinion and yet remain within the bounds of the confession. The assembly's exchange might sound like the worst sort of postmodern reading of a text, where authorial intent is irrelevant and the individual's interpretation reigns supreme. On the contrary, the divines were deliberately ambiguous on this point. They incorporated doctrinal flexibility into the document to accommodate a pluriform orthodoxy. They recognized that the purpose of a confession of faith is to codify the corporate faith of the church; it is not to be a manifesto that binds every individual on every doctrinal question.

A second illustration comes from the confession's chapter on the covenants. A simple reading of the confession gives the impression that the divines were united in their affirmation of the covenant of works. From one vantage point, this is true. The confession states, "The first Covenant made with Man, was a Covenant of Works, wherein Life was promised to Adam, and in him to his posterity, upon condition of perfect and personal obedience" (7.2). But this is also another instance of methodical ambiguity written into the confession. The confession merely states that God promised Adam "life." It does not say "eternal life." This was no oversight; it was intentional. There was a debate among the members of the assembly regarding the precise nature of Adam's reward. Thomas Goodwin (1600–1680) contended that Adam's reward was entirely natural; God offered him extended life in the garden. Leviticus 18:5 promised only

---

18. Chad Van Dixhoorn, ed., *Minutes and Papers of the Westminster Assembly, 1643–1653*, 5 vols. (Oxford: Oxford University Press, 2012), sess. 520, 3:689–90.

19. *The Humble Advice of the Assembly of Divines, Now by Authority of Parliament Sitting at Westminster, Concerning a Larger Catechism* (London, 1648). This original does not number the catechism questions, so I employ the common numbering for ease of reference.

long life in the land, not eternal life. Pre-fall Sabbath days were only types of heaven. And because God published the moral law through the law of nature, it mentions nothing of heaven.[20] Others, such as Samuel Rutherford, argued the opposite case. Rutherford maintained that God promised Adam the reward of heavenly communion.[21] As he understood it, Leviticus 18:5 held out the prospect of eternal life. Theologians of the period based this conclusion on intracanonical exegesis of Leviticus 18:5; that is, they coordinated this Old Testament text with Christ's use of it.[22] When a lawyer asked Jesus what he must do to inherit eternal life, Jesus referred him to the law and asked him what it said (Luke 10:25–26). The lawyer responded with the two greatest commandments: to love God and to love neighbor (Luke 10:27; Lev. 19:18; Deut. 6:4–6). To this answer, Christ replied, "You have answered correctly; do this, and you will live" (Luke 10:28; see also Lev. 18:5). The lawyer asked about the way to gain eternal life, and Christ pointed him to Leviticus 18:5. These theologians believed that the same principle was at work in the garden when God gave Adam the command; Adam's reward, therefore, was eternal life.

The divines found themselves at an impasse and determined that the best way forward was principled ambiguity. The confession's intentionally unspecific use of the word *life* allowed theologians of both opinions to embrace the statement.[23] In other words, Goodwin and Rutherford could both affirm that Adam's reward was *life*, but the vagueness of the term allowed each theologian to qualify it to suit his particular convictions: extended life in the garden for Goodwin and eternal life for Rutherford.

A third illustration comes from the confession's treatment of assurance. There were variations of opinion regarding the proper

20. Thomas Goodwin, *Of the Creatures, and the Condition of Their State by Creation* 2.6, in *The Works of Thomas Goodwin*, 12 vols. (Eureka, CA: Tanski Publications, 1996), 7:49–50.

21. Samuel Rutherford, *The Covenant of Life Opened: Or, A Treatise of the Covenant of Grace* 1.9 (Edinburgh, 1654), 49.

22. See, e.g., David Dickson, *Truths Victory over Error* (Edinburgh, 1684), 137–39.

23. Mark A. Herzer, "Adam's Reward: Heaven or Earth?," in *Drawn into Controversie: Reformed Theological Diversity and Debates Within Seventeenth-Century British Puritanism*, ed. Michael A. G. Haykin and Mark Jones (Göttingen: Vandenhoeck & Ruprecht, 2011), 162–82.

formulation of the doctrine of assurance. John Calvin (1509–64) notably claimed that assurance was of the essence of faith, whereas the Westminster Confession takes a slightly different view: "This infallible assurance doth not so belong to the essence of faith" (18.3). There were different views among theologians of the Reformed tradition as well as a diversity of opinions among the members of the assembly. The confession does not give a specific explanation as to how, for example, a person receives assurance; it provides only a general theological framework: "A true believer may wait long, and conflict with many difficulties before he be partaker of it: yet, being inable by the Spirit to know the things which are freely given him of God, he may, without extraordinary revelation, in the right use of ordinary meanes, attain thereunto" (18.3). The confession only states that through the use of ordinary means a person can attain assurance of salvation, yet it does not specify what those ordinary means are. Some might claim that the Larger Catechism identifies these ordinary means as word, sacraments, and prayer (q. 154). This claim has a degree of truth to it, but it does not reveal the whole picture. The divines left this statement undefined because they did not agree on the precise means that a person might use to attain assurance.[24] They were not in agreement regarding the precise role of the *syllogismus practicus* (practical syllogism), for example.[25]

What conclusions can one draw regarding these deliberately ambiguous statements on the decree, the covenant of works, and assurance? There are three important observations about the compromise regarding the phrasing of the statement on the covenant of works. First, the statement codified the assembly's broad agreement regarding the covenant of works. Second, their agreement and statement were not so strict as to rule out different variations on the doctrine. The confession does not leave itself open to only one version of the doctrine of the covenant of works but at least two, if not more. Third, Rutherford

24. Jonathan Master, *A Question of Consensus: The Doctrine of Assurance after the Westminster Confession* (Minneapolis: Fortress, 2015), 61–66, 77–79.

25. Master, *Question of Consensus*, 134–36. The *syllogismus practicus* teaches that believers may determine whether they are saved because only believers produce good works: Believers produce good works. I produce good works, therefore I am a believer. On this issue, see Richard A. Muller, *Calvin and the Reformed Tradition: On the Work of Christ and the Order of Salvation* (Grand Rapids: Baker Academic, 2012), 244–76.

and Goodwin had diametrically opposed exegesis at certain points, as is evident in their contradictory interpretations of Leviticus 18:5. The Westminster divines were agreed on most doctrinal conclusions, but they often took different exegetical paths to reach those conclusions. Confessions were never intended to confine the church to one overly defined theological position on every issue. The best confessions have doctrinal flexibility built in, to make room for differing opinions on challenging topics. Moreover, the fact that the divines were initially reticent to attach proof texts to the confession does not reveal a lack of exegesis; rather, it shows that they did not all agree on the best scriptural paths to various doctrinal conclusions.[26] One can observe the differences of opinion emerge by comparing Westminster Confession 18.2 with its parallel statement in the Savoy Declaration:

Westminster Confession of Faith 18.2 (1646)	Savoy Declaration 18.2 (1658)
This certainty is not a bare conjectural and probable persuasion, grounded upon a fallible hope; but an infallible assurance of faith, founded upon *the divine truth of the promises of salvation*, the inward evidence of those graces unto which *these* promises are made, the *testimony* of the Spirit of adoption *witnessing with our spirits that we are the children of God; which Spirit is the earnest of our inheritance, whereby we are sealed to the day of redemption.*	This certainty is not a bare conjectural and probable persuasion, grounded upon a fallible hope; but an infallible assurance of faith, founded on *the blood and righteousness of Christ, revealed in the gospel, and also upon* the inward evidence of those graces unto which promises are made, *and on the immediate witness of the Spirit,* testifying our adoption, *and as a fruit thereof, leaving the heart more humble and holy.*

Some believed that the Spirit employed the Word of God to assure believers, and others held that the Spirit *immediately* witnessed to them (i.e., witnessed directly; *without mediation*, either by Scripture or by anything else). Both views arguably fall under the category of "ordinary means," but the absence of either in the Westminster

---

26. Garnet Howard Milne, *The Westminster Confession of Faith and the Cessation of Special Revelation: The Majority Puritan Viewpoint on Whether Extra-Biblical Prophecy Is Still Possible* (Eugene, OR: Paternoster, 2008), 11–13.

Confession reveals that the divines did not want to adjudicate the matter in the document.[27]

This doctrinal flexibility warrants the observation that there are unique rules for interpreting confessions of faith. Unlike the Scriptures, for which interpreters seek the intent of the human authors and ultimately of the divine author, confessions are consensus documents, for which readers have to recognize the range of theological opinion standing behind and accommodated by them. When reading a biblical text, one deals with two authors (a divine and a human). When reading a confession, however, one may be dealing with any number of authors. Heinrich Bullinger (1504–75) wrote the Second Helvetic Confession (1566) all on his own, whereas more than one hundred theologians and pastors were involved in the composition of the Westminster Standards (1648).[28] Authorial intent takes on a different cast when there are multiple authors with contradictory opinions. Hence, when interpreting a confession, one must account for three different interpretive categories. Readers must distinguish between what is confessional, contra-confessional, and extra-confessional.

To say that the Scriptures teach the covenant of works is to make a confessional claim. The affirmation stands in harmony with the confession. To say, on the other hand, that God justifies sinners by faith and good works is to make a contra-confessional claim. This affirmation stands in contradiction to the clear teaching of the confession. These are the two categories that most clergy employ. But the third is equally necessary, both historically and ecclesiologically. To say that God promised Adam only extended life in the garden as his reward or to say that there is one divine decree rather than multiple would be to make an extra-confessional claim. This means that a confession's omissions can, at times, be just as important as its explicit statements. The Westminster divines purposefully created space for extra-confessional opinions and did not seek to smother them. The only time an extra-confessional view might come under censure is if it conflicts with the explicit teaching of the confession. This means that confessions draw both lines and circles. They draw lines that the church must not cross to distinguish orthodoxy from

27. Master, *Question of Consensus*, 156.
28. Pelikan and Hotchkiss, *Creeds*, 2:458–59.

heresy and to preserve the faith once delivered to the saints. But they also draw circles, areas of doctrinal freedom where adherents may hold a number of variant positions and still be within the bounds of orthodoxy.

Codifying the Church's Historic Witness

One of the most important benefits of a confession of faith is that it ideally captures and preserves the church's historic witness to Christ. As the first chapter argued, we must stand on the shoulders of giants in order to catch a glimpse of the glory of the triune God. The apostle Paul makes it clear that Christ has given gifts to the church in the form of apostles, prophets, evangelists, shepherds, and teachers (Eph. 4:11). With the closing of the canon and the cessation of divine revelation (Eph. 2:20), we must distinguish between inspired and uninspired teaching. This means that the church must always subordinate its confessions to the authority of God's Word—the only rule in doctrine, faith, and life. But at the same time, Protestant churches face the challenge of historical myths about the nature of the Reformation that work against these biblical and confessional impulses.

It is a popular notion that the Reformation was a complete break with the medieval past, but this narrative does not fit well with the historical evidence. True, early Reformation-era theological works often left important topics unaddressed. Philipp Melanchthon's 1521 edition of his *Loci Communes*, for example, does not address the doctrine of the Trinity. But he included the vital topic in subsequent editions.[29] There were some early impulses to shy away from the church's earlier doctrinal pronouncements, but this did not last long. In the face of the exigencies created by the Roman Catholic Church, the Reformers had to clarify their positions regarding church tradition.

In the early days of the Reformation, Roman Catholic officials tried to stop the ecclesiastical hemorrhaging. They wanted to halt the exodus

29. Philipp Melanchthon, *Loci Communes Theologici (1521)*, in *Melanchthon and Bucer*, ed. Wilhelm Pauck, LCC (Philadelphia: Westminster, 1969); Melanchthon, *The Chief Theological Topics: Loci Praecipui Theologici 1559*, 2nd ed., trans. J. A. O. Preus (St. Louis: Concordia, 2011), 10–39; Richard A. Muller, *Post-Reformation Reformed Dogmatics*, 4 vols. (Grand Rapids: Baker Academic, 2003), 4:143.

from the Roman fold and regain lost churches. Roman Catholic bishop Jacopo Sadoleto (1477–1547) believed that he could entice the Reformed churches back into the Roman church through dialogue, and so he dispatched a letter to Geneva in an effort to appeal to them.[30] He warned the Genevans of the dangers of the novel doctrine they had erroneously embraced. Was it wise or expedient, he asked, to shred fifteen hundred years of church doctrine and replace it with "innovations introduced within these twenty-five years, by crafty, or, as they think themselves, acute men; but men certainly who are not themselves the Catholic Church?"[31] Sadoleto raised two charges: that the Reformation was fueled by doctrinal novelty and that it was sectarian—in other words, that theologians who were not part of the church fabricated novel doctrines to lead the faithful of Rome away into error. But was the Protestant Reformation truly sectarian and of recent origins?

Calvin responded to Sadoleto's charge of novelty in a letter that reportedly took him six days to craft.[32] Should the Genevans follow the authority of the established church or listen to the "inventors of new dogmas"?[33] Calvin refuted the allegation by setting forth his definition of the church: "The society of all the saints, a society which, spread over the whole world, and existing in all ages, yet bound together by the one doctrine, and the one Spirit of Christ, cultivates and observes unity of faith and brotherly concord."[34] Calvin's definition of the church is the root of his response to the charge of novelty; it is a definition that grows out of the soil of his theology and branches into two main claims: that the Reformation churches stand within the one, universal Christian tradition leading back to the apostles and that the Roman churches have deviated from that tradition in a number of specific ways.

30. Bruce Gordon, *Calvin* (New Haven: Yale University Press, 2009), 96; Jacopo Sadoleto, *Epistola ad Senatum Populumque Genevensem, que in Obedientiam Romani Pontificis Eos Reducere Conatur. Ioannis Calvini Responsio* (Argentor, 1539).

31. Jacopo Sadoleto, "Cardinal Sadolet's Letter to the Senate and People of Geneva," in *John Calvin: Tracts and Letters*, ed. and trans. Henry Beveridge, 7 vols. (1851; repr., Edinburgh: Banner of Truth, 2009), 1:14.

32. Gordon, *Calvin*, 96.

33. John Calvin, "Reply by John Calvin to Cardinal Sadolet's Letter," in *John Calvin: Tracts and Letters*, 1:36.

34. Calvin, "Calvin to Cardinal Sadolet," 37.

Given that Calvin argued that the church extended to people all over the world and throughout every age, he did not believe that the Reformed churches arose *de novo* in the sixteenth century. The Reformed churches had a historical foundation that reached to the earliest days of the church. In particular, the list of theologians that Calvin invoked as part of his historical foundation included Chrysostom (ca. 347–407), Basil of Caesarea (329–79), Cyprian (ca. 200–258), Ambrose (ca. 339–97), and Augustine (354–430). These were all theologians that Sadoleto would undoubtedly claim for Rome, but Calvin believed that the Reformed churches were more closely aligned with their teaching than the sixteenth-century Roman church was.[35] Claiming these theologians for the Reformation would have been hollow were it not for the fact that Calvin and the Reformers readily and frequently appealed to patristic theologians in their works. This was a practice that Reformed theologians carried on well into the period of High Orthodoxy (1640–1700).[36] Calvin appealed to the catholicity of the Reformed church. He, therefore, substantively argued that he and his peers were Reformed *catholics*, part of the church universal spread throughout the world and in every age. In matters of doctrine, Calvin claimed, "We hesitate not to appeal to the ancient Church."[37]

When Calvin addresses the differences between the Reformed and Roman churches, one should note the specific issues that he raises: doctrine, discipline, sacraments, and ceremonies.[38] When he provides the details for these four categories, he largely dwells on two *loci* of theology: soteriology and ecclesiology. Calvin, for example, identifies the doctrine of justification as "the first and keenest subject of controversy between us."[39] Justification rests in the cradle of soteriology, but this doctrine also touches matters related to anthropology. Under the locus of ecclesiology, Calvin focuses on the sacraments (especially the eucharist) and church authority.[40]

---

35. Calvin, "Calvin to Cardinal Sadolet," 38.
36. Irena Backus, ed., *The Reception of the Church Fathers in the West*, 2 vols. (Leiden: Brill, 2001), 2:573–699, 839–88.
37. Calvin, "Calvin to Cardinal Sadolet," 39.
38. Calvin, "Calvin to Cardinal Sadolet," 38.
39. Calvin, "Calvin to Cardinal Sadolet," 41.
40. Calvin, "Calvin to Cardinal Sadolet," 39–41, 45–55.

Calvin's comments are significant both in what he does and in what he does not state. He flags the issues of difference—soteriology and ecclesiology—but he does not seek out other points of conflict. This means that other loci—such as prolegomena, theology proper, Christology, or eschatology—were not greatly disputed.[41] Moreover, if Calvin extended the Reformed church to the patristic era, then this also meant that he was willing to accord the ecumenical councils a degree of authority within the Reformed churches. The Reformers did not scuttle the ecumenical councils; rather, they accepted them because they agreed with Scripture, and the Reformers gave them authority in the church subordinate to the authority of Scripture. Evidence of the acceptance of the ecumenical creeds appears in a number of major Reformed confessions and catechisms that either endorse or echo the creedal language.[42]

The Westminster Standards, for example, employ the formulas of the ancient catholic creeds. Despite the claims of some who argue that the Westminster Standards present a distinctly nonspeculative, *Reformed* rather than *catholic* Christology, the Larger Catechism nevertheless affirms Nicaea's statements regarding the eternal generation of the Son:

Q. How many persons are there in the God-head?

A. There is but three Persons in the God-head, the Father, the Son, and the Holy Ghost, and these three are one true, eternal God, the same in substance, equal in power and glory; although distinguished by their Personal Properties.

Q. What are the Personal Properties of the three Persons in the God-head?

A. It is proper to the Father to beget the Son, and the Son to be begotten of the Father, and to the Holy Ghost to proceed from the Father and the Son, from all eternity. (qq. 9–10)[43]

41. Muller, *Calvin and the Reformed Tradition*, 51–58.
42. Tetrapolitan Confession, 2; First Helvetic Confession, 3; Belgic Confession, 8–11; Second Helvetic Confession, 2–3; Thirty-Nine Articles, 1, 8; Irish Articles, 7–10.
43. Cf. Robert L. Reymond, *A New Systematic Theology of the Christian Faith* (Nashville: Thomas Nelson, 1998), 325–26; Robert Letham, "Review of Robert Reymond, *A New Systematic Theology of the Christian Faith*," *Westminster Theological*

And numerous statements from the confession's chapter on Christ (8) echo the ecumenical creeds—including Nicaea (325), Constantinople (381), Ephesus (431), and Chalcedon (451).[44] The Second London Confession aptly expresses the thought behind the agreement with and use of ancient creedal formulas: "We have no itch to clogg Religion *with new words*, but do readily acquiesce in that form of sound words, which hath been in consent with the holy Scriptures, used by others before us."[45]

Heiko Oberman (1930–2001) explained that the Reformers never completely scuttled tradition. He helpfully distinguished between *tradition 1* and *tradition 2*. Protestants, representing *tradition 1*, had a single source of authority: Scripture. And Roman Catholics, representing *tradition 2*, had two sources: Scripture and tradition.[46] Protestants identified Scripture as their sole authority but did not dispense with tradition. Rather, they consulted and employed tradition, but always as a resource subordinate to Scripture. Protestant theologians were quite comfortable and even desirous to identify themselves as Reformed catholics. That is, they believed they were part of the one catholic church and wanted to prove their organic connection to it. The Westminster Standards swim in this stream, as do most Protestant confessions. The standards codify ancient creeds and join hands with the church throughout the ages to profess the faith once delivered to the saints.

The Westminster divines were catholic. That is, they believed they were the true heirs of the universal church and the Roman Catholic Church had deviated from truth. In the words of Herman Bavinck (1854–1921), "Irenaeus, Augustine, and Thomas [Aquinas] do not belong exclusively to Rome; they are Fathers and Doctors to whom the whole Christian church has obligations. Even the post-Reformation Roman Catholic theology is not overlooked. In general, Protestants

---

Journal 62 (2000): 314–20; Chad Van Dixhoorn, "Post-Reformation Trinitarian Perspectives," in *Retrieving Eternal Generation*, ed. Fred Sanders and Scott R. Swain (Grand Rapids: Zondervan, 2017), 180–207.

44. Fesko, *Westminster Standards*, 184.

45. *A Confession of Faith: Put Forth by the Elders and Brethren of Many Congregations of Christians* (London, 1688), preface, fols. A6r–A7v.

46. Heiko A. Oberman, *The Harvest of Medieval Theology: Gabriel Biel and Late Medieval Nominalism* (Cambridge, MA: Harvard University Press, 1963), 371–72.

know far too little about what we have in common with Rome and what divides us."[47] That is, the tree trunk of the one true church runs from the postapostolic period through the Reformation. Rome represents a deviating branch, not the Protestant Reformation. Thus, as with other Protestant confessions, the Westminster divines incorporated numerous catholic teachings that had roots in the ancient church.

At the same time, the divines also made use of existing confessional documents to create their own. Some of the divines were schooled in the Heidelberg Catechism (1563), and they carried this knowledge with them into the assembly's deliberations.[48] In their debates, the divines referred to both the Canons of Dort (1619) and the Second Helvetic Confession (1566).[49] But the most used document was the Irish Articles (1615), written by James Ussher, the archbishop of Armagh. The divines gleaned much from the Irish Articles, at times borrowing significant sections, albeit slightly reworded.[50] All of this points to the fact that the divines were advocates of what Oberman would later call *tradition 1*; they were in no way endeared to *tradition 0*. *Tradition 0* rejects all forms of tradition and claims the Bible as the sole authority; rather than *sola Scriptura* (Scripture alone), it promotes *solo Scriptura* (Scripture only).[51]

47. Herman Bavinck, "Foreword to the First Edition (Volume 1) of the *Gereformeerde Dogmatiek*," trans. John Bolt, *Calvin Theological Journal* 45 (2010): 9–10.

48. R. Scott Clark and Joel Beeke, "Ursinus, Oxford, and the Westminster Divines," in *The Westminster Confession into the Twenty-First Century*, ed. J. Ligon Duncan (Fearn: Mentor, 2004), 2:1–32.

49. Van Dixhoorn, *Minutes and Papers*, 1:154, 159.

50. See Alan Ford, *James Ussher: Theology, History, and Politics in Early-Modern Ireland and England* (Oxford: Oxford University Press, 2007), 85–103; B. B. Warfield, "The Westminster Doctrine of Holy Scripture," in *The Works of Benjamin B. Warfield*, ed. E. D. Warfield et al., 10 vols. (1931; repr., Grand Rapids: Baker, 1981), 6:169–90.

51. Mark Noll, "Chaotic Coherence: *Sola Scriptura* and the Twentieth-Century Spread of Christianity," in *Protestantism after Five Hundred Years*, ed. Mark Noll and Thomas Albert Howard (Oxford: Oxford University Press, 2016), 274–75. Too many Protestants mistakenly believe that *sola Scriptura* means that there is little to no place for church tradition in the life and doctrine of the church. But a view that rejects all tradition, *solo Scriptura* (Scripture only), devolves into an individualistic biblicism in which people cease to read and interpret the Scriptures in concert with the church throughout the ages.

Conclusion

Confessions have many benefits for the church, but chief among them are distinguishing between orthodoxy and heterodoxy, maintaining boundaries for a diversified orthodoxy, and codifying the historic witness of the church. As beneficial as these things are, they are not the automatic fruit of adopting a confession. There are three corresponding responsibilities that foster and preserve these three benefits. First, the church must never take doctrinal truth for granted. Dead traditionalism and formalism are always looming dangers for the church. Each generation must make a personal appropriation of the corporate confessional faith of the church. Only when the next generation studies the dividing lines between orthodoxy and heterodoxy can they appreciate and profess their doctrinal heritage. The present-day church must confess the living faith of the dead, not the dead faith of the living.[52] Only with a firm understanding of the faith of their ancestors will they persevere in this dedication to truth. Christians must realize that the dividing lines are not an end unto themselves but ultimately must lead to a humble faith in and worship of our triune God. Orthodox confessions will never suffice to keep a church on the path of truth; only our faithful triune God can do this. But the confessions of the church are one of the means by which he accomplishes this goal.

Second, as the Christian-influenced mores and norms of Western culture collapse around us, the church undoubtedly hears the siren call of fundamentalism. The call for a diversified orthodoxy likely scares some and may even look like the poison of liberalism and doctrinal compromise. Undoubtedly, we must confess the same corporate faith; but we must, at the same time, allow room for a diversified orthodoxy. In his assessment of the Westminster Standards, John Murray (1898–1975) observed, "To demand acceptance of every proposition in so extensive a series of documents would be . . . dangerously close to the error of placing human documents on par with holy Scripture."[53] The framers of the Westminster Standards

52. Jaroslav Pelikan, *The Vindication of Tradition* (New Haven: Yale University Press, 1984), 43.
53. John Murray, "Creed Subscription in the Presbyterian Church in the USA," in *The Subscription Debate: Studies in Presbyterian Polity*, ed. Morton Smith (Greenville, SC: Greenville Presbyterian Theological Seminary, n.d.), 79.

included doctrinal flexibility at points to allow for a diversified ortho-doxy. If churches do not allow for a range of acceptable opinions on certain matters, there are two likely consequences: churches will atrophy because of inflexibility, with gifted clergy and laypeople seeking other contexts in which to serve, and many who assent to the prescribed opinions will do so only formally, or even deceptively. As B. B. Warfield (1851–1921) once commented, "Overstrictness de-mands and begets laxity in performance" and "dishonesty lurks."[54] In other words, ministers would simply utter the doctrinal shibboleths to pass ordination exams or perhaps even resort to deception. An ecclesiologically sanctioned, variegated orthodoxy, however, allows for different convictions and exegesis while maintaining established doctrinal boundaries.

Third, and finally, churches can only truly appreciate the historic witness of their confessions if they are intimately familiar with these documents. Due in part to ignorance and to the passing of time, there are many corners of our confessional documents that contain impor-tant doctrinal truths that are lost on contemporary churches. Several trends are to blame. Some look only to a small cadre of twentieth-century theologians to define the Reformed tradition. Others do slightly better but trace their faith back only to the sixteenth century. They fail to recognize the catholicity of the Reformed confessions, that the framers of Protestant confessions affirmed doctrines that have medieval and patristic roots. A perusal of the works of John Calvin (1509–64), Francis Turretin (1623–87), or John Owen (1616–83), for example, quickly reveals critical interaction with patristic and me-dieval authors. This means that churches need to alter their reading habits and become better acquainted with theologians who lived prior to the sixteenth century. Such a reading diet will preserve the catholic-ity of the Reformed churches for future generations.

---

54. B. B. Warfield, "Presbyterian Churches and the Westminster Confession," *Presbyterian Review* 10, no. 40 (1889): 648–49.

FIVE

Confessions and Piety

Introduction

Killing and confessions seem like strange bedfellows. But in one small corner of church history, the two almost went hand in hand. During the Synod of Dort (1618–19), one of the delegates was so angered by his colleague that he challenged him to a duel to the death. Writing confessions can be a difficult process because people care about the church's doctrine and want to contend zealously for truth. But gather any group of Christians together and disagreement will undoubtedly arise. How should we resolve such disagreements? How should we conduct ourselves when others upset us? The "duel that almost was" provides the opportunity to study the relationship between confession writing and piety or, more broadly, the connection between doctrine and practice. Through the window of this event, we will see that even in their most theological moments (such as writing confessions), Christians must not allow the world to shape the church's ethos and conduct. The "duel that almost was" also highlights our continual need for Christ and living out our union with him.

The first section presents a brief biographical sketch of the chief character in the drama, Franciscus Gomarus. One's upbringing, personal experiences, and convictions inform one's decisions, both good and bad. The second section explores the infamous event—the specific doctrinal dispute and situation that led to Gomarus throwing down the gauntlet. The third section concisely explores the topic of duels. One of the necessary components for accurately assessing this incident is understanding early modern culture and how dueling was a common means of resolving conflicts. One must not approach this situation with twenty-first-century feelings and opinions about dueling. This is not to say that dueling is acceptable; on the contrary, it is sinful, and many early modern theologians believed it was immoral. But not every theologian believed it was wrong to duel. Thus, we must explore seventeenth-century theology to see why dueling was considered by some to be an acceptable practice. Understanding the early modern context and the prevalence of dueling sets the stage for the fourth section of the chapter, which examines the biblical reasons why ministers at the synod rejected dueling. Fifth, and finally, the chapter reflects on the practical lessons this infamous incident presents for the church.

The Man

Franciscus Gomarus (1563–1641) is perhaps little known today, but he was very well known in the sixteenth and seventeenth centuries. He was renowned for his diligent work to extirpate the teachings of his colleague Jacob Arminius (1560–1609).[1] Gomarus's devotion to the Reformed faith was undoubtedly fostered by his personal experience and suffering. Gomarus's family was from the city of Bruges in the Flemish region of what is now Belgium. Since Roman Catholic Spanish armies occupied Bruges, when Gomarus converted to the

1. The following biographical sketch relies on Michael A. Hakkenberg, "Gomarus, Franciscus," in *The Oxford Encyclopedia of the Reformation*, ed. Hans J. Hillerbrand, 4 vols. (New York: Oxford University Press, 1996), 2:181–82; and Simon J. Kistemaker, "Leading Figures at the Synod of Dort," in *Crisis in the Reformed Churches: Essays in Commemoration of the Great Synod of Dort, 1618–19*, ed. Peter Y. De Jong (1968; repr., Grandville, MI: Reformed Fellowship, 2008), 57–72, esp. 61–64.

Reformed faith in the late 1570s, he was forced to flee to the Palatinate. This flight indubitably impressed upon his mind the importance of his theological convictions. Gomarus learned Latin and Greek, and when he was fourteen years old, he commenced his studies at Strasbourg. Between 1582 and 1584, he studied at Oxford and Cambridge. In 1585, Gomarus left England for Neustadt and Heidelberg. In 1587, he was called from Heidelberg to serve as the pastor of a Reformed Walloon refugee congregation in Frankfurt. And in 1594, he moved to the University of Leiden to serve as a professor of theology.

During his time at Leiden, Gomarus engaged in theological debate with his colleague Arminius and with Arminius's successor, Conrad Vorstius (1569–1622). Gomarus debated Arminius over the doctrines related to predestination and justification. He also confronted Vorstius over his doctrine of the Trinity. The outcome of these debates was unsatisfactory to Gomarus, however, which likely motivated his resignation from Leiden in 1611. He served briefly as a pastor of the Reformed church in Middelburg and then took up a second teaching post at the seminary in Saumur, France, from 1614 to 1618. He concluded his career at the University of Groningen. Gomarus represented the University of Groningen at the Synod of Dort, where he was a vocal critic of Remonstrant theology. In fact, in the initial stages of the controversy, the debate parties were known as Arminians and Gomarists. (They would only later be referred to as Remonstrants and Contra-Remonstrants.)[2] Gomarus was a man of many talents and experiences: a religious refugee, a theological student who studied under some of Europe's greatest minds, a pastor, and a theological professor.

Because of his pastoral experience, Gomarus was not an ivory tower academic. He had to interact with people who were going through difficult and trying circumstances. The plague was a continual threat.[3] In fact, in 1602 the plague took the lives of two of Gomarus's colleagues at Leiden, which is what led to Arminius's appointment. Gomarus's first wife, Emerentia, died in childbirth

---

2. Anthony Milton, ed., *The British Delegation and the Synod of Dort (1618–1619)* (Suffolk, UK: Boydell, 2005), xvii.

3. William Naphy and Andrew Spicer, *Plague: Black Death and Pestilence in Europe* (Gloucestershire, UK: The History Press, 2011), 77–102.

along with their first child in 1591, very shortly after they were married. At a number of points during the Synod of Dort, Gomarus expressed concern that they write the canons in a pastoral rather than an academic, or scholastic, manner.[4] At the same time, Gomarus could be truculent and obnoxious. Francis Junius (1545–1602), a fellow colleague at the University of Leiden who was related to him by marriage, wrote of Gomarus, "That man pleases himself most wonderfully by his own remarks. He derives all his stock of knowledge from others; he brings forward nothing of his own: or, if at any time he varies from his usual practice, he is exceedingly infelicitous in those occasional changes."[5]

While his writings and labors were extensive and covered a wide range of topics, historians and theologians perhaps know him best for his views on predestination.[6] He did not merely debate Arminius over the doctrine of predestination; he went to great lengths to alert other churches and universities of Arminius's aberrant doctrinal views.[7] Nevertheless, Gomarus biographers note that he did not take a prominent position at the synod; he avoided publicity and sought to work peacefully with his fellow delegates. When Remonstrant theologian Simon Episcopius (1583–1643) took the floor, for example, Gomarus remained quiet and only once spoke to deny the charge that the Reformed taught absolute reprobation. At another point, Gomarus even intervened on behalf of some of the "less obstinate" Remonstrants and pleaded that the synod treat them mercifully.[8] But it seems that Gomarus was more patient with and willing to suffer his theological foes than he was his friends.[9]

4. Milton, *British Delegation*, 195.
5. As quoted in Herman Hanko, *Portraits of Faithful Saints* (Grandville, MI: Reformed Free Publishing Association, 1999), 321.
6. See, e.g., Jacob Arminius, *Examination of the Theses of Dr. F. Gomarus Respecting Predestination*, in *The Works of James Arminius*, trans. James Nichols and William Nichols, 3 vols. (Grand Rapids: Baker, 1986), 3:521–658.
7. Aza Goudriaan, "Justification by Faith and the Early Arminian Controversy," in *Scholasticism Reformed: Essays in Honour of Willem J. van Asselt*, ed. Maarten Wisse, Marcel Sarot, and Willemien Otten (Leiden: Brill, 2010), 155–78.
8. Milton, *British Delegation*, xl; Gerard Brandt, *History of the Reformation and Other Ecclesiastical Transactions in and about the Low-Countries*, 3 vols. (London: 1722), 3:282.
9. Kistemaker, "Leading Figures," 62–63.

The Incident

After the synod dismissed the Remonstrants from the proceedings, Gomarus engaged in a debate with fellow delegate Matthias Martinius (1572–1630). John Hales (1584–1656), synodical observer and chaplain to the English ambassador Sir Dudley Carleton (1573–1632), wrote a letter to Carleton dated January 15, 1618, in which he detailed the exchange between Gomarus and Martinius. The synod debated matters related to the first head of doctrine (i.e., to predestination) on the evening of January 12, 1618. The delegates discussed the question of whether Christ was the *fundamentum electionis* (foundation of election) and, if so, in what manner.[10] When debate broke out on the floor of the synod, the apparently quiet and demure Gomarus could not hold his peace. Hales observed, "Others brookt none of those Restraints. D. *Gomarus* stands for the former sentence, and in defence of it had said many things on Friday." Hales avers that Martinius voiced his objections to Gomarus's views: "This night *Martinius* of *Breme* being required to speak his mind, signified to the synod, that he made some scruple concerning the Doctrine passant about the manner of Christs being the *Fundamentum Electionis*, and that he thought Christ not only the Effector of our Election, but also the Author and procurer thereof."[11] Thus far the exchange presented as a routine debate, as two theologians expressing their disagreement with each other. But things were about to explode.

Hales does not give every detail, but Martinius must have expressed himself in an objectionable way. He may have cast aspersions on Gomarus or somehow insulted him because Gomarus objected strenuously.

> *Gomarus* who owes the Synod a shrewd turn, and then I fear me began to come out of debt; presently, as soon as *Martinius* had spoken, starts up, and tells the Synod, *ego hanc rem in me recipio* ["I take this charge to myself"], and therewithal casts his Glove, and challenges *Martinius* with

---

10. John Hales to Sir Dudley Carleton, 15 January 1618, in *Golden Remains, of the Ever Memorable, Mr. John Hales*, 2nd ed., 2 vols. (London, 1673), 2:86–88. All subsequent references to Hales's letter come from this source. This letter also appears in Arminius, *Works of James Arminius*, 1:512–13n.

11. Hales to Carleton, *Golden Remains*, 2:87.

this Proverb, *Ecce Rhodum, ecce saltum* ["Here is your test, show yourself courageous"], and requires the Synod to grant them a Duel, adding that he knew *Martinius* could say nothing in refutation of that Doctrine.[12]

Gomarus took offense at Martinius's arguments and challenged him to a duel. He believed that Martinius could not refute his doctrine and thus resorted to insults. So Gomarus met his affront with an opportunity for Martinius to demonstrate his courage in a duel to the death. Whether they would use pistols or rapiers is unclear, as both were common weapons of choice. But Martinius, Hales tells us, "easily digested the affront," and "after some few words of course, by the wisdom of the *praeses* ["presider," or "moderator"] matters seemed to be a little pacified, and so according to the custom, the Synod with Prayer concluded."[13] One might think that corporate prayer signaled that all were pacified, but this was not the case. After the prayers concluded, "Zeal and Devotion had not so well allayed *Gomarus* his choler, but immediately after Prayers he renewed his Challenge and required Combat with *Martinius* again; but they parted for that night without blowes."[14] So prayer could not extinguish the fires of Gomarus's temper; but fortunately for all, they went their separate ways (whether voluntarily or involuntarily is unclear).

Hales explains that the next morning the English delegation met with Martinius in private to discuss his doctrinal views and his conduct.[15] The English delegation was concerned that Martinius's views were favorable toward Remonstrant positions; this was a concern shared by a number of the Dutch representatives, including Gomarus.[16] The English divines sought to win him over to common Reformed views on these subjects. Martinius was unpersuaded, but "he promised moderation and temper in such manner, that there should be no dissention in the Synod by reason of any opinion of his."[17]

---

12. Hales to Carleton, *Golden Remains*, 2:87.
13. Hales to Carleton, *Golden Remains*, 2:87.
14. Hales to Carleton, *Golden Remains*, 2:87.
15. *Acta et Documenta Synodi Nationalis Dordrechtanae (1618–1619)*, ed. Donald Sinnema, Christian Moser, and Herman J. Selderhuis, vol. 1, *Acta of the Synod of Dordt* (Göttingen: Vandenhoeck & Ruprecht, 2015), lxxviii–lxxix.
16. Milton, *British Delegation*, 215.
17. Hales to Carleton, *Golden Remains*, 2:87–88.

Martinius promised he would not create controversy, but historical records show that he and Gomarus and other delegates vigorously debated issues. The deliberations, however, never became as acrimonious as they did on the evening of January 12, 1618.[18]

Attitudes toward Dueling

To most readers, the fact that Gomarus sandwiched the synod's closing prayer with his two challenges to face Martinius in a duel looks scandalous. Bookending prayer with lethal threats hardly seems defensible. However, one must approach this incident not with twenty-first-century sensibilities but with a critical and historically sympathetic evaluation of the events that transpired that evening. This is not to excuse sinful conduct in the participants but, rather, to assess the situation fairly and not impose anachronistic norms on past events. There are three things to consider in such a contextual evaluation: the political and theological stakes for the outcome of the synod, duels as a common early modern means of resolving conflict, and theological opinions on the morality of dueling.

Political and Theological Stakes

We live in an age that does not take theology as seriously as earlier generations. As some observers have commented, we live in a disenchanted world where people no longer perceive a direct connection between God and daily life.[19] Hence, doctrinal disputes are no more than coffee-shop banter. But such was not the case in early modern Europe. Not only was the world still enchanted, but theology, politics, and war were also inextricably intertwined. That King James

18. Gomarus and two other delegates, Sibrandus Lubbertus (ca. 1556–1625) and Abraham Sculetus (ca. 1585–1625), repeatedly criticized Martinius for his use of Jesuit scholastic terminology, which was a source of acrimony between them. See Milton, *British Delegation*, xxvi, xlv, 208, 213; Donald Sinnema, "Reformed Scholasticism and the Synod of Dort (1618–19)," in *John Calvin's Institutes: His Magnum Opus*, Proceedings of the Second South African Congress for Calvin Research, ed. B. J. van der Walt (Potchefstroom: Institute for Reformational Studies, 1986), 467–507, esp. 476–80, 483–87.

19. Charles Taylor, *A Secular Age* (Cambridge, MA: Harvard University Press, 2007), 25–89.

(1566–1625) personally dispatched the English delegation to the synod is evidence of the fact that political authorities of the highest rank had great interest in the outcome. The Dutch Reformed churches lived with the constant threat of war and Spanish occupation. The commingling of theological and physical conflict would burst upon the European scene in a matter of months in what became known as the Thirty Years' War (1618–48), one of the bloodiest and most devastating conflicts in human history. For delegates like Gomarus, doctrine influenced politics, and his memories of refugee life certainly haunted him. The synod occurred just before the execution by beheading of Johan van Oldenbarnevelt (1547–1619), the Land's Advocate of Holland who supported the Remonstrants. In the wake of the synod, noted theologian and Remonstrant supporter Hugo Grotius (1583–1645) was imprisoned. And among the outcomes of the synod was the formal conviction of the Remonstrants, which included their prohibition from preaching on pain of banishment and confiscation of property.[20] As a result, many Remonstrant ministers fled the Netherlands. In this historical context, sadly, theology and death often went hand in hand. This is not to say that dueling was therefore legitimate, but it was not seen as especially out of place. These theologians lived and debated in a period when violence was often a by-product of confessions of faith, so Gomarus challenging a colleague to a duel would not have been immediately suspect.

Duels as Common to Early Modernity

A second contextual factor is how ordinary duels were in this time. In early modern Europe, dueling was a regular part of life, dating back at least to the patristic period. David beat Goliath in a duel, and God vindicated the anointed king-to-be; many believed this constituted exegetical support for dueling. "During the combat, God awaits, the heavens open, and He defends the party who he sees is right."[21] In 501, Gundebald (d. 516), king of the Burgundians, formally per-

20. Jonathan I. Israel, *The Dutch Republic: Its Rise, Greatness, and Fall 1477–1806* (Oxford: Clarendon, 1995), 450–65; Milton, *British Delegation*, xvii.
21. Barbara Holland, *Gentlemen's Blood: A History of Dueling. From Swords at Dawn to Pistols at Dusk* (New York: Bloomsbury, 2007), 9.

mitted duels as a judicial tribunal (trial by combat).[22] In the Middle Ages, even though some objected to the practice, dueling continued to enjoy overall public acceptance.[23] Duels in this period took the form of noblemen fighting with swords or jousting on horseback. By the sixteenth century, one of the most common reasons that men engaged in duels was to defend their honor. Scholarly estimates for the twenty-one-year reign of Henry IV (1553–1610) of France place the national death toll from dueling as high as ten thousand. This is approximately 476 dueling deaths per year, which means that for two decades, nearly ten men fell in duels every week. These numbers included noblemen and even clergy.[24] Why was the death toll so high? It did not take much to incite a duel in the seventeenth century. Calling someone a liar, either directly or merely by insinuation, was enough. Sir Walter Raleigh (1552–1618) once wrote in his famous poem, *The Lie*, "To give the lie / Deserves no less than stabbing."[25] Despite the penchant for and popularity of dueling among the general population, civil law and the church frowned on the practice. But when two men engaged in a duel and one killed the other, the winner was put on trial but usually acquitted on the grounds of self-defense. The judge in the trial might declare that the accused conducted himself in a manner worthy of a "man of honor."[26] William Shakespeare (1564–1616) captures the seventeenth-century estimation of dueling, and the importance of honor, in the words of Iago, the villain of *Othello*:

> Good name in man and woman, dear my Lord
> Is the immediate jewel of their souls; who steals my purse
>   steals trash;
> 'tis something, nothing; 'Twas mine, 't's his, and has been a
>   slave to thousands;

22. Holland, *Gentlemen's Blood*, 9; François Billacois, *The Duel: Its Rise and Fall in Early Modern France* (New Haven: Yale University Press, 1990), 15.

23. Holland, *Gentlemen's Blood*, 10.

24. Holland, *Gentlemen's Blood*, 22–23; see also Mark Greengrass, *Christendom Destroyed: Europe 1517–1648* (New York: Viking, 2014), 133–34.

25. Holland, *Gentlemen's Blood*, 40; V. G. Kiernan, *The Duel in European History* (Oxford: Oxford University Press, 1989), 48; Walter Raleigh, *The Works of Sir Walter Raleigh*, vol. 8 (Oxford: Oxford University Press, 1829), 726; see also Billacois, *The Duel*, 8–9.

26. Holland, *Gentlemen's Blood*, 87, 89.

> But he that filches from me my good name
> Robs me of that which not enriches him,
> And makes me poor indeed.[27]

Iago's good name and his honor were more valuable than his possessions and were worth defending at all costs, even worth risking a duel to the death. If Raleigh's poem and Iago's declaration are any indication, all Gomarus had to believe was that Martinius had insinuated that he was a liar, and even that would have been a sufficient offense to warrant dropping the glove.

Opinions on the Morality of Dueling

There were obviously some theologians and ministers who believed that dueling was an acceptable, if nevertheless unfortunate, way to resolve conflicts. The fact that Gomarus was willing to duel Martinius is prima facie proof of this fact. Nonetheless, this does not mean that everyone shared this view. That the English delegation intervened to smooth things over and that the synod did not grant Gomarus's request demonstrate that most believed dueling was, at minimum, politically unadvisable and, at maximum, downright immoral. That is, at one level, the synod did not want the political trouble that would come with having dueling on the agenda as a means by which their delegates resolved theological differences. Delegates shooting or dicing each other with swords is bad optics; the world was watching, and this kind of thing might have given the Remonstrants the upper hand in winning the hearts and minds of the Dutch people. On another level, there were those who believed that dueling was immoral, such as fellow delegate to the synod John Davenant (1572–1641).

Davenant directly addresses this topic in his commentary on Colossians 3:13 ("bearing with one another and, if one has a complaint against another, forgiving each other; as the Lord has forgiven you, so you also must forgive").[28] In his exegesis of this verse, Davenant

---

27. William Shakespeare, *Othello*, act 3, sc. 3, lines 128–71, in *William Shakespeare: Complete Plays* (New York: Fall River, 2012), 836; James Bowman, *Honor: A History* (New York: Encounter Books, 2006), 56; Kiernan, *The Duel*, 56.

28. John Davenant, *An Exposition of the Epistle of St. Paul to the Colossians*, 4th ed., 2 vols. (London, 1831).

draws on insights from Bernard of Clairvaux (1090–1153), who argued that Christology should be the doctrinal foundation for defining Christian virtues.[29] In this particular case, Christ forgives sinners of their transgressions, therefore Christians should forgive one another. Davenant lists four points by which Christians should compare their own conduct with Christ's:

1. Christians must be keenly aware of the degree of their own sin, and conversely the depth of the forgiveness they have received from Christ. Such knowledge informs the Christian's willingness to forgive others.
2. The one who is unwilling to forgive others does not personally know Christ's forgiveness.
3. Christians vainly excuse their own revengeful malice regardless of how great they believe they have suffered wrong. Moreover, even if one suffers a wrong, it does not mean that his character has automatically been impugned. All such claims and notions vanish in light of Paul's statement, "as the Lord has forgiven you, so you also must forgive."

Davenant's fourth point is worth quoting in full, as he directly addresses the question of dueling, revealing that it was common and accepted among the upper classes:

4. It is, therefore, a diabolical opinion, which has possessed the minds of almost all those who lay claim to gentility, that they cannot bear, even a reproachful word, without the loss of their honour and their reputation; but are under the necessity of seeking revenge in a duel, at the manifest peril of their own lives, and a plain attack upon the life of another.[30]

Davenant then moves into a second phase of his argument in which he appeals to pagan authorities to support his claim that Christians should be willing to suffer wrongs.[31] In his *Gorgias*, Socrates (ca.

---

29. Davenant, *Colossians*, 2:115; see also Bernard of Clairvaux, *On the Song of Songs*, serm. 22.11, vol. 1 (Trappist, KY: Cistercian Publications, 1971), 103.
30. Davenant, *Colossians*, 2:116.
31. Davenant, *Colossians*, 2:116–17.

470–399 BC) states that every injury is dishonorable to the inflictor, not to the one who suffers it.[32] In his *Nicomachean Ethics*, Aristotle (384–322 BC) presents the same view: "To inflict injury is the effect of dishonesty; and on that account dishonorable and infamous: but to suffer one with equanimity is the effect of virtue, and therefore glorious."[33] The Roman Stoic philosopher Seneca (ca. 4 BC–AD 65) similarly opines: "We ought to despise injuries, and what I may call the shadow of injuries, contumely, whether they fall deservedly or undeservedly upon us. If deservedly, it is not contumely, but judgment given; if undeservedly, it is for him who did the injury, and not for me to be ashamed of it."[34] But as true as these pagan sentiments are, and as much as they generally confirm his point, Christ's teaching was decisive for Davenant: "Blessed are you when others revile you and persecute you" (Matt. 5:11).

In a third phase, Davenant gives three specific reasons why dueling is sinful. He prefaces his reasons with the statement that, even if one suffers injury, it does not therefore follow that one may lawfully repel the injury by means of a duel. Davenant's three reasons are as follows:

1. No one should be the judge in his own cause, let alone when anger, violence, and passion mark him. In his work, *Concerning Patience*, Tertullian (160–220) writes: "What have I to do with a passion, which I cannot govern through impatience?"[35]
2. Christians do injury to God and his magistrate when they seek revenge by private means: "Vengeance is mine, and recompense" (Deut. 32:35; Rom. 13:14). Paul instructs the church that the magistrate does not bear the sword in vain, but he would be superfluous if God intended for individuals to draw the sword at their own pleasure.
3. Those who duel meet every offense with the same punishment, namely, death. This is not the verdict of a generous

32. Socrates, *Gorgias*, in *Plato: The Collected Dialogues*, ed. Edith Hamilton and Huntington Cairns (Princeton: Princeton University Press, 1961), 252–54.
33. Aristotle, *Nicomachean Ethics* 5.11, 2nd ed., ed. Terrence Irwin (Indianapolis: Hackett, 1999), 84–85.
34. Seneca, *On the Resolute Nature of the Wise Man* 16.3, in *Selected Dialogues and Consolations*, ed. and trans. Peter J. Anderson (Indianapolis: Hackett, 2015), 33.
35. Tertullian, *Of Patience* 10, in *Ante-Nicene Fathers*, vol. 3 (Grand Rapids: Eerdmans, 1993), 714.

man, but a madman. Punishments should be commensurate with the offense.[36]

Davenant presents one last argument by appealing to Christ's teaching in Matthew 26:52, "For all who take the sword will perish by the sword," and Augustine's interpretation of it—namely, that those who take the law into their own hands without having legitimate and divinely appointed authority will fall either by the sword of worldly violence or by the sword of divine vengeance.[37] Davenant concludes his exegesis of Colossians 3:13 with one final observation worth quoting in full:

> From all these reasons it appears clear, that they are absolutely madmen, who follow the opinions of the man, renouncing the doctrine of Christ: so that they may retain the name of Gentlemen, they do not fear the title of homicide; and, finally, so that they may avoid suspicion of false infamy, they leap into the very pit of hell itself. Thus much of those virtues which we practice towards such persons as are hostile and injurious to us.[38]

Davenant, therefore, believed that even though dueling was a commonly accepted practice, it was immoral and should be rejected.

There are at least three points worthy of observation in Davenant's rejection of dueling. First, Davenant was present when Gomarus challenged Martinius to a duel. His arguments against dueling, therefore, were likely shaped by the events of that dreadful night. Second, even though dueling was common in the sixteenth and seventeenth centuries, its cultural acceptability did not automatically legitimate it. Third, there are similarities between Davenant's rationale for rejecting duels and the pagan reasons for suffering wrong, but there is also a big difference between them. For Socrates, Aristotle, or Seneca, personal pride or principles of Stoic virtue were the goal of being willing to suffer wrongs. For Davenant, one's submission to God's

---

36. Davenant, *Colossians*, 2:117.
37. Davenant, *Colossians*, 2:118; see Augustine, *Our Lord's Sermon on the Mount* 2.19.62, in *Nicene and Post-Nicene Church Fathers*, vol. 6, ed. Philip Schaff (Grand Rapids: Eerdmans, 1996), 55.
38. Davenant, *Colossians*, 2:118.

authority was at stake. He believed that willingness to suffer wrong was the result of sanctification ultimately rooted in union with Christ. Willingness to suffer injury was, for Davenant, the chief means by which Christians revealed how well they understood the doctrine of Christ and the forgiveness of their sins. Pagan ethics and cruciform virtues may look similar, but in reality they are worlds apart. The former is the faint echo of the original, unsullied image of God now marred by sin; the latter emanates from the glorious brilliance of the Son and the new heavens and new earth.

The Lessons

The "duel that almost was" serves as a perennial warning to all Christians. It teaches us two lessons in particular: (1) that we need to be on guard lest the world press the church into its mold and (2) that we need to ground our conduct in our union with Christ.

Being on Guard against Worldliness

Ministers may no longer draw pistols at dusk, but they do nevertheless throw down the gauntlet in other ways. All too often the vitriolic rhetoric of politics seeps into the church. The same is true of discourse on the internet. Theological debates on social media unfortunately read all too much like the heated exchanges that transpired between Gomarus and Martinius. Tempers flare, hearts seethe, and fingers type harsh words that fly through cyberspace and inflict damage on the souls of fellow Christians. Some are all too willing to traffic in gossip and rumor in their efforts to win a theological dispute—victory at any cost.

Many do not realize how much social media and technology shape their conduct. Psychologist and neuroscientist Maryanne Wolf documents the commonsense dynamic that the more a person is exposed to a particular medium, the more that medium influences and forms them.[39] Wolf's chief concern is how technological mediums such as

---

39. Maryanne Wolf, *Reader, Come Home: The Reading Brain in a Digital World* (New York: Harper, 2018), 107.

screens transform the mind and adversely affect one's reading habits. She links the detrimental effects of internet and screen reading to the loss of critical thought and deep-reading capacity. As readers' attention spans shrink, so does their interest in reading serious books. As readers pivot away from serious books because they demand too much intellectual bandwidth and do not deliver the stimulation of other forms of media, they lose the capacity for empathy. Recent studies conducted at Stanford University reveal a 40 percent decline in empathy in young people over the last two decades, a degeneration directly linked to online reading and a lack of real-time, face-to-face relationships.[40]

What happens to people when they stop reading books that place them outside of their own world and give them the experience of walking in someone else's shoes? Wolf recounts the experience of a young Catholic boy reading Anne Frank's *Diary*. The book enabled him to have a life-changing encounter with a young Jewish girl's tragic experience of persecution, hatred, and ultimately death.[41] The loss of such deep-reading encounters has played a role in Western culture's regression into incivility and cruelty where people no longer view one another as fellow citizens and human beings but as the "sinister other."[42] Sadly, the slash-and-burn vitriol of the internet has swallowed both culture and church in a dark cloud of negativity and immorality. The more Christians use the internet, the more it reshapes both their minds and their conduct. In simpler terms, you become what you worship. Visit many Christians' social media pages and you will see that backbiting, sarcasm, and verbal cruelty abound. Tempers are short, and rebukes fast and furious. Many Christians think little about forwarding emails and posting tweets that amount to nothing more than tasty morsels of gossip. Such posts may win many "likes" and "retweets," but the words of Proverbs should echo in our ears: "When words are many, transgression is not lacking, but whoever restrains his lips is prudent" (Prov. 10:19). True, words do less physical damage than the rapier's blade or the pistol's lead slug, and they may therefore seem harmless. But bullets, swords, and words are all

40. Wolf, *Reader, Come Home*, 50.
41. Wolf, *Reader, Come Home*, 48.
42. Wolf, *Reader, Come Home*, 47.

signs of the disposition of one's soul. Whether or not deadly force is used, God looks at the nature of a person's heart: "But I say to you that everyone who is angry with his brother will be liable to judgment; whoever insults his brother will be liable to the council; and whoever says, 'You fool!' will be liable to the hell of fire" (Matt. 5:22).

Thus, Christians should take special care and not allow the world to press them into its mold—especially in how they conduct the business of the church, and even in things as seemingly innocuous as the words they use. As Christians engage in debate, they must do so ever mindful of how the world around them might be shaping their conduct. As Paul writes, "Do not be conformed to this world, but be transformed by the renewal of your mind, that by testing you may discern what is the will of God, what is good and acceptable and perfect" (Rom. 12:2). Will technology make the church a place of quarreling, anger, hostility, gossip, and disorder (cf. 2 Cor. 12:20)? The book of Proverbs has much to say about the words we use: "Whoever belittles his neighbor lacks sense, but a man of understanding remains silent" (Prov. 11:12). Likewise, "A gentle tongue is a tree of life, but perverseness in it breaks the spirit" (Prov. 15:4). Our words—whether in speech, in print, or on the internet—should be a source of life rather than of enmity or strife: "The words of a man's mouth are deep waters; the fountain of wisdom is a bubbling brook" (Prov. 18:4). A commitment to being careful with our words does not mean that we should never rebuke or correct. But we need to ask ourselves, Can we strike a clean blow? When cutting out sin, must we always use the lumberjack's chainsaw, or could we employ the surgeon's scalpel instead? As Paul writes, "Brothers, if anyone is caught in any transgression, you who are spiritual should restore him in a spirit of gentleness. Keep watch on yourself, lest you too be tempted" (Gal. 6:1). We must be vigilant against being conformed to the patterns of the world so that our words may always be a fountain of life, wisdom, and love. Vigilance against sin, however, is only half of the sanctification equation.

Grounding Our Conduct in Our Union with Christ

Christians cannot merely rely on their own determination to conquer besetting sin, even if empowered by the Holy Spirit. God does not call us to the avoidance of sin but to the positive manifestation of the righteousness of Christ; the only fount of this righteousness is Christ, and thus union with him is of the greatest importance. We should etch Paul's words on our hearts: "I have been crucified with Christ. It is no longer I who live, but Christ who lives in me. And the life I now live in the flesh I live by faith in the Son of God, who loved me and gave himself for me" (Gal. 2:20). We do not merely lay hold of the power of Christ or the Spirit to combat our sin and reshape our nature; rather, we possess the indwelling presence of the resurrected Christ by virtue of our union with him.[43] Our conversion, then, is not mere moral improvement but a radical re-creation so that we can bear the image of Christ.[44] Paul reminds the Christians in Ephesus: "You . . . were taught in him [Jesus] . . . to put off your old man, which belongs to your former manner of life and is corrupt through deceitful desires, and to be renewed in the spirit of your minds, and to put on the new man, created after the likeness of God in true righteousness and holiness" (Eph. 4:21–24, trans. mine). We are to do the same. Our "old man" is our former existence in Adam, the first man; and our "new man" is our new existence in Christ, the *eschatos* man, the last Adam (1 Cor. 15:45). "Just as we have borne the image of the man of dust, we shall also bear the image of the man of heaven" (1 Cor. 15:49).

Bernard of Clairvaux highlights our absolute and desperate need for union with Christ:

> What have you to do with righteousness if you are ignorant of Christ, who is the righteousness of God? Where, I ask, is true prudence, except in the teaching of Christ? Or true justice, if not from Christ's mercy? Or true temperance, if not in Christ's life? Or true fortitude, if not in Christ's Passion? Only those can be called prudent who are imbued with his teaching; only those are just who have had their sins pardoned through his mercy; only those are temperate who take pains to follow his way of life; only those are courageous who hold fast to the example of his patience when buffeted by sufferings. Vainly therefore will anyone strive to acquire the virtues, if he thinks they may be

---

43. Grant Macaskill, *Living in Union with Christ: Paul's Gospel and Christian Moral Identity* (Grand Rapids: Baker Academic, 2019), 56.

44. Macaskill, *Union with Christ*, 1.

obtained from any source other than the Lord of the virtues, whose teaching is the seed-bed of prudence, whose mercy is the well-spring of justice, whose life is a mirror of temperance, whose death is the badge of fortitude.[45]

Soteriology must always look to Christology as its lodestar. In particular, Christians must keep the cross of Christ ever before them. As the worldly waves of incivility, anger, and impatience crash down upon us, our souls remain tranquil because we rest upon the rock of Christ, who by his Spirit enables us to respond with patience, love, and kindness. Or in some cases, we might even choose to remain silent. In the cacophonous waterfall of words that flow off our screens, silence might actually speak volumes. Our silence in the face of insults publicly manifests our union with Christ.

Christ's cross reminds us of our sinfulness and unworthiness as well as of the forgiveness that has come through him, but it also leaves a cruciform impression on all that we do. When reviled, we do not respond in kind; when falsely accused, we do not resort to vengeance; and when justice delays her verdict or even fails to appear, we lay our injuries at the foot of the cross and rejoice that we were counted worthy to share in his sufferings. Martinius's offense against Gomarus may have been grievous. Gomarus's truculent spirit may have been overly sensitive. Whatever the case may be, Gomarus missed an opportunity to share in the sufferings of Christ when he dropped his glove and challenged Martinius to a duel. Gomarus saw the way of the cross as weak and demanded immediate vindication. May we instead, through the abiding presence of Christ, find the strength to manifest patience, kindness, and love when we encounter impatience, cruelty, and fear. May we never trade the narrow way of the cross for the fleeting carnal satisfaction of the broad and easy path of vengeance.

Conclusion

The "duel that almost was" is an embarrassing episode in the life of the church. While only two delegates were involved in the kerfuffle,

---

45. Bernard of Clairvaux, *Song of Songs*, serm. 22.11, 103.

the fact that hundreds of years later the historical record still lays bare their impiety is a sad memorial. Nevertheless, rather than bury, forget, or ignore such sins, we should own them. Only when we own the sins of the past can we learn from our mistakes. We should never fear acknowledging mistakes; rather, it is not learning from them that should make us tremble. In this case, we must always recognize that sin lies crouching in our hearts, ready to pounce on our godliest intentions, and this is especially true when it comes to writing confessions of faith. We must always, therefore, seek to live out our union with Christ and continually ask whether we have unwittingly allowed the world to shape our conduct. This is especially true when dealing with high-stakes doctrine and confession writing. High stakes do not warrant elevated tempers but instead call for ascending prayers beseeching God's grace to help us live in a godly manner. Our desire in every debate should be to shed the light of truth rather than to bring the heat of discord. Our goal must be to promote the truth, not to win arguments. As chapter 1 explained, confessions and piety go hand in hand. Even when tempers flare in our efforts to write confessions of faith, we must keep the love of God and neighbor ever before us. How can we write of the mercy of God in our confessions and then instantly forget it because a colleague or friend—or enemy—disagrees with us? Again, confessions and piety must always go hand in hand. The words of our confessions must rise off the page and take on the flesh of concrete acts of Christian virtue—of faith, hope, and love. Otherwise, our confessions become tombstones of a dead tradition rather than testimonies of the church's living faith in our triune God.

Conclusion

Confessions of faith may rub against the individualistic grain of our present culture, but history testifies to their enduring necessity and value. The Bible commends confessions to the church so that through them believers might meditate on the truth, digest it, and pass it on to future generations. Some have complained that creeds and confessions have become more detailed and restrictive; they compare, for example, the Apostles' Creed with the Belgic or the Westminster Confession. The Bible does not specify how detailed or how long a confession should be. These things fall under the category of wisdom. Nevertheless, the exponential growth of false teaching requires the church to be more specific regarding the truths it professes. Some will point to the convulsive violence that marred the seventeenth-century landscape after the creation of new confessional boundaries. Does such violence automatically invalidate the confessional project? In my judgment, it does not. After the bloodshed of the seventeenth century, theologians and ministers in ecclesiastical bodies reexamined the relationship between church and state and determined that the church should not bear the sword. A most welcome correction! This change to confessional documents also demonstrates that Reformed confessional churches are willing and able to make necessary modifications to their confessions in order to bring them into greater alignment with Scripture.

In our present cultural climate, the siren call to minimize the church's confessional commitments is strong. The underlying assumption is that churches need to make concessions to the ever-changing culture in their efforts to attract the masses. The desire to evangelize the lost is certainly a noble and biblically righteous cause. But how the church goes about its mission is just as important as the mission itself. A confession of faith functions as a theological spine, holding a body of doctrinal truths upright. Apart from this vital infrastructure, churches become vulnerable to every wind of doctrine, disconnected from their theological past, and open to organizing the church around cults of personality or the worst sort of fundamentalism rather than around the teaching of Scripture: the gospel of Christ. Through confessions of faith, we can practice the democracy of the dead and consult the wisdom of ages past as we press forward toward the future—as we embrace the truth in the present and pass it on to our children. Despite the waning influence of confessions of faith in the present, there are brighter days still ahead for confessionalism. There is still, therefore, a need for creeds today.

For Further Reading

Confessional Documents and Collections

The Canons and Decrees of the Council of Trent. Translated by H. J. Schroeder. Rockford, IL: Tan Books, 1978. First published 1941 by B. Herder Book Co. (St. Louis).

A Confession of Faith: Put Forth by the Elders and Brethren of Many Congregations of Christians. London, 1688.

The Humble Advice of the Assembly of Divines, Now by Authority of Parliament Sitting at Westminster, Concerning a Confession of Faith. London, 1647.

The Humble Advice of the Assembly of Divines, Now by Authority of Parliament Sitting at Westminster, Concerning a Larger Catechism. London, 1648.

Kelly, J. N. D. *Early Christian Creeds.* 3rd ed. New York: Routledge, 1982.

Kolb, Robert, and Timothy Wengert, eds. *The Book of Concord: The Confessions of the Evangelical Lutheran Church.* Minneapolis: Fortress, 2000.

Lumpkin, William L., and Bill J. Leonard. *Baptist Confessions of Faith.* 2nd rev. ed. Valley Forge, PA: Judson, 2011.

Pelikan, Jaroslav, and Valerie Hotchkiss, eds. *Creeds and Confessions of the Faith in the Christian Tradition.* 4 vols. New Haven: Yale University Press, 2003.

Schaff, Philip. *The Creeds of Christendom.* 3 vols. Grand Rapids: Baker, 1990.

Sinnema, Donald, Christian Moser, and Herman J. Selderhuis, eds. *Acta et Documenta Synodi Nationalis Dordrechtanae (1618–1619)*. Vol. 1, *Acta of the Synod of Dordt*. Göttingen: Vandenhoeck & Ruprecht, 2015.

Torrance, T. F. *The School of Faith: The Catechisms of the Reformed Church*. Eugene, OR: Wipf & Stock, 1996. First published 1959 by Clarke (London).

Van Dixhoorn, Chad, ed. *Minutes and Papers of the Westminster Assembly, 1643–1653*. 5 vols. Oxford: Oxford University Press, 2012.

The Westminster Confession of Faith. Glasgow: Free Presbyterian Publications, 1995. First published 1646 (London).

Zanchi, Girolamo. *De Religione Christian Fides—Confession of Christian Religion*. Edited by Luca Baschera and Christian Moser. 2 vols. Leiden: Brill, 2007.

Secondary Sources

Chesterton, G. K. *Orthodoxy: The Romance of Faith*. New York: Doubleday, 1990. First published 1908 by John Lane (London).

Clark, R. Scott. *Recovering the Reformed Confession: Our Theology, Piety, and Practice*. Phillipsburg, NJ: P&R, 2008.

Fairbairn, Donald, and Ryan M. Reeves. *The Story of Creeds and Confessions: Tracing the Development of the Christian Faith*. Grand Rapids: Baker Academic, 2019.

Fesko, J. V. *The Theology of the Westminster Standards: Historical Context and Theological Insights*. Wheaton: Crossway, 2014.

Goudriaan, Aza, and Fred van Lieburg, eds. *Revisiting the Synod of Dort (1618–1619)*. Leiden: Brill, 2011.

Jedin, Hubert. *A History of the Council of Trent*. 2 vols. London: Thomas Nelson and Sons, 1963.

Letham, Robert. *The Westminster Assembly: Reading Its Theology in Historical Context*. Phillipsburg, NJ: P&R, 2009.

Milton, Anthony, ed. *The British Delegation and the Synod of Dort (1618–1619)*. Suffolk, UK: Boydell, 2005.

Murray, John. "Creed Subscription in the Presbyterian Church in the USA." In *The Practice of Confessional Subscription*. Edited by David W. Hall, 301–21. 3rd ed. Powder Springs, GA: Covenant Media Foundation, 2018.

O'Malley, John W. *Trent: What Happened at the Council*. Cambridge, MA: Belknap, 2013.

Pelikan, Jaroslav. *Credo: Historical and Theological Guide to Creeds and Confessions of Faith in the Christian Tradition.* New Haven: Yale University Press, 2005.

———. *The Vindication of Tradition.* New Haven: Yale University Press, 1984.

Trueman, Carl R. *The Creedal Imperative.* Wheaton: Crossway, 2012.

Ursinus, Zacharias. *The Commentary of Dr. Zacharias Ursinus on the Heidelberg Catechism.* Phillipsburg, NJ: Presbyterian and Reformed, n.d.

Van Dixhoorn, Chad. *Confessing the Faith: A Reader's Guide to the Westminster Confession of Faith.* Edinburgh: Banner of Truth, 2014.

Warfield, B. B. "Presbyterian Churches and the Westminster Confession." *Presbyterian Review* 10, no. 40 (1889): 646–57.

Wengert, Timothy J. *The Augsburg Confession of Faith: Renewing Lutheran Faith and Practice.* Minneapolis: Fortress, 2020.

Scripture Index

Subject Index